Become All That God Has Created You To Be

Kehinde Adesina
with
Taiwo Adesina

ISBN: 978-1-909787-29-2

Published by Purpose2Destiny TK Limited

All scripture quotations are taken from the New King James Version (NKJV) unless otherwise indicated.

Other scriptures used are The New International Version (NIV) and The Amplified Bible (AMP)

(Small letter "s" is used in satan and not capitalized so as not to glorify him)

Dedication

To our Most Righteous God and Father – we thank You for Your Mercy, Faithfulness and Love towards us; prior to the discovery of who You created us to be we only existed, but now we live.

To our late parents – Prince Gabriel Olusanjo and Mrs Bolajoko Adesina who were used as instruments in God's hands to birth children of purpose.

To Chief Prince Solomon Mofolusho (late) and Mrs. Adeola Adesina, we thank you for your support and counsel through the years. We pray that God will continue to strengthen and uphold your families.

To our spiritual parents – Pastors Mathew and Yemisi Ashimolowo, who awakened God's purpose in us, may God fulfil your hearts desires and cause all that He has planned for you to come to pass speedily.

To our brothers – Pastor Adebowale, Adeyemi and Oluyinka Adesina; and Godchildren – Olumuyiwa Sholagbade, Toluwalase Ademola, Yla Punchi, Zra Punchi and Eden Alidor and their families, may you all manifest what God has stored inside of you; may your light shine before men.

To our family and friends – may God continue to bless and keep you and cause you to walk in His calling and purpose for your lives; may you all fulfil destiny.

Acknowledgement

We thank our brother, Pastor Adebowale Adesina for his encouragement, insight, input and guidance given to us during the completion of this book.

We also thank Georgina Chong-You, who contributed towards the successful completion of this book and Jumoke Ademola of Gemsjummy Photography.

Table of Contents

Introduction

God "created" Man. God made Man in His own image, likeness and design. He made them male (Adam) and female (Eve) and placed His seed within them. Out of them spread abroad a multitude of men and women who have since walked the face of the earth. God created man for a particular purpose: to manifest His Glory and to be Godlike. As a child of God you too carry God's Seed within you and you have been created and ordained for a particular purpose.

Adam forgot why he was created and fell into sin; likewise many of his posterity failed to understand God's purpose for their lives and they aborted their destiny. Despite the fall, the Bible tells us that some men and women recognised their calling and fulfilled their life's purpose. Although they faced challenges and made mistakes along the way they overcame and lived victoriously.

Our life is a journey of purpose, started by God. It is however our responsibility to ensure that we continue this journey in Him. There are many who feel that they have no purpose to fulfil in life, they feel they fell from outer space into this world we call "earth" and they wonder what they should be doing with their lives. We too grew up feeling this way! We felt lost, hopeless and purposeless; we however took inspiration from the written testimonies of the men and women in the Bible who rose up and made a difference in their generation.

As a result of receiving God's enlightenment of our purpose, we are now walking in our calling. We have written this book to inform those who want to know what their purpose in life is; for those who want to discover who they are in God and for those who have entered into that understanding but want to maximise their potential in order to fulfil their destiny.

Whilst the testimonies of those who succeeded in fulfilling their life's purpose should be of great inspiration to you, you must also learn from those who made mistakes. Their mistakes, faults and weaknesses should be a warning to you that you must keep God in the driver's seat of your life. You need God's Spirit to lead you through your life's journey. You can only have the Spirit of God guiding you when you have welcomed Jesus Christ into your life. With this "Trinity Factor", you are on course to becoming all that God has created you to be.

As you read this book, we pray that you will receive the revelation of who God has created you to be from conception, so that you can take hold of all that He has in store for you.

CHAPTER 1

God's Intention for Man at Creation

"In The Beginning God" created the heavens and the earth, light and every other living thing. On the sixth day He created Man. This Biblical narrative indicates that man was created by God. The Christian belief follows this hypothesis that it was God and no other who set the process of creation into motion and directed its course. Man was God's most valuable creation as God had high expectations for him. In the beginning of time, God took the centre stage in creating man because only He could perfect what He saw in His Spirit. This is confirmed to us in *Genesis 1: 26-31 (Amp) which says:*

> 'God said, Let Us [Father, Son, and Holy Spirit] make mankind in Our image, after Our likeness, and let them have complete authority over the fish of the sea, the birds of the air, the [tame] beasts, and over all of the earth, and over everything that creeps upon the earth. So God created man in His own image, in the image and likeness of God He created him; male and female He created them. And God blessed them and said to them, Be fruitful, multiply, and fill the earth, and subdue it [using all its vast resources in the service of God and man]; and have dominion over the fish of the sea, the birds of the air, and over every living creature that moves upon the earth.'... And God saw everything that He had made, and behold, it was very good (suitable, pleasant) and He approved it completely. And there was evening and there was morning, a sixth day.

The Lord God formed Man from the dust of the ground, breath and life entered into Man and Man became a living being (Genesis 2:7). From the beginning you can see God's approval of His creation, for what He created was fitting, good and pleasant. God created man to be special and unique; there was no match or equal for man on earth and in the heavens, not even the angels ministering and serving before God. Genesis 1:31 states that when God saw that everything He had made was very good He approved of them completely. This shows that God had accomplished His purpose for us on the day of our Creation so He rested on the seventh day. God rested because He had made man complete in Himself to live a fulfilling and productive life.

In Genesis 1, God used the words, "image, likeness, dominion, and dominate". Defining these words will enlighten you about God's intentions for you and for all mankind (definitions are taken from Your Dictionary.com)

1) **"Let us make mankind in our own image, after our likeness."** – God created man in His own image and likeness; He therefore expects us to be like Him in everything and in every way.

IMAGE – (NOUN)

- An imitation or representation of a person or thing, drawn, painted, photographed.

- The visual impression of something produced by reflection from a mirror, refraction through a lens, etc.

- A person or thing very much like another; copy; counterpart; likeness.

LIKENESS – (NOUN)

- Resemblance

- Outward appearance: *humans are made in God's likeness*
- A portrait or representation.

The word "Man" means Adam in the Hebrew language. God created Adam in His own image and therefore Adam was expected to manifest the true image of God, he was not created to become a duplicate, counterfeit or carbon copy of another person. Adam was expected to be like God in all his ways.

Genesis 1: 27 states, "God created man in His own image, male and female, He created them." Although some tend to joke that women were only an after thought on God's mind and were made of inferior material, this is not the case! God definitely thought about women by making "Eve" in His own image, Genesis 2:18, 21-23 states that God created "woman" to be a helper to Adam and she was complementary to his life.

God created you to have character and colour in your life. You have been made according to God's design and not from a previous copy or product already in existence. God – The Father, Son and Holy Spirit sat down and designed you to function as a person. God knew where to place your head, eyes, nose, vital organs and legs within your frame. You are Godlike and God is your foundation. You were made from God's perceptive; you should therefore see yourself from His perceptive and not your own or men's. You are clothed with God's dignity, righteousness and holiness.

2) **"Let them have complete authority and dominion over all His creation"** – God created man to have complete authority and dominion, He expects us to walk in the authority and dominion He has given us.

DOMINION - (NOUN)

- The power or right of governing and controlling; sovereign authority. Rule; control; domination.

- A territory, usually of considerable size, in which a single rulership holds sway. Lands or domains subject to sovereignty or control.

DOMINATE - (NOUN)

- An act or instance of dominating.

- Rule or sway; control, often arbitrary.

Although God created man to have authority, He expects man to be dependent on Him. God gave complete authority to man to exercise lordship, power and dominion over all things. Genesis 1:26; 29 says that God made Man to have dominion over all the works of His Hands and He put all things under his feet.

In times past, kings and emperors reigned with absolute authority over their kingdoms and subjects to enact laws and decrees as they deemed fit. Adam named every other creation as he had the power and authoritative word in his mouth, whatever he called them, they became. Often people are given power and authority to do things with limitations; however, God gave man complete power and authority that cannot be curtailed in any manner or form (Genesis 2:19-20).

In Psalms 82:6 God says that, "we are gods and we are all children of the Most High," therefore the word of oracle has been placed in our mouths to command what we want without fear, doubt or hesitation. If we are gods then we have authority over satan himself provided we remain attached to God.

If we are gods we must also begin to act, talk and walk like one. I am not saying we should idolise ourselves but rather we must stand straight and upright with confidence like Kings and Emperors. How do people treat royalty? We know they are treated with honour, reverence and respect; likewise we too deserve that honour by reason of the pronouncement God has bestowed upon us. God has freely given us so many things and He expects us to take possession of them.

In Genesis 1, God also used the words "Fruitful, Multiply, Good, Pleasant and Approved" defining these words would also enlighten you better about God's intentions for you and for all mankind (definitions are taken from The Compact Oxford English Dictionary-3rd Edition)

3) **"Let them be fruitful and multiply; fill the earth and subdue it"** – God created man to be fruitful, to multiply and to fill the earth, He expects us to be productive in whatever we do.

FRUITFUL –(ADJ.)

- Producing much fruit; fertile.
- Producing good results; productive

MULTIPLY – (VERB) - MULTIPLIES, MULTIPLIED

- Increase in number or quantity
- Increase in number by reproducing

God's blessing of fruitfulness means that whatever you lay your hands on will result in fruitfulness and productivity. You won't be able to hide the results of your blessings as they will overflow and overspill for all to see. God's blessings will make you profitable in all your endeavours. You would produce good, tangible and exceptional results. You have been created to be fertile and you are earmarked for success. You will surely become useful, purposeful and effective.

You have been commissioned to multiply and to increase to such an extent that the world will have no choice but to take notice of you. You have been commissioned to produce a hundred fold return in whatever you sow (Mark 10:30). Not only will you multiply on your own account, all those around you will also reap from your Godly fortune. You would produce protégés to become achievers like yourself. God wants us to multiply in every area of our lives. God expects you to fill the earth with all that He has bestowed on you. He has filled you up so that you can in turn pour out everything deposited inside of you. He expects you to impart your world, become a blessing to your family and to your generation.

You have been made complete from the time of your conception and therefore no matter how much you give, you would always be full. God's blessings in your life cannot run dry. God owns the entire universe and all that is in it (Psalms 24:1); He owns all the resources on earth, which He has made available to us. He expects us to make use of everything that grows on the ground for our nourishment and benefit, He expects us to subdue the earth by taking charge of its resources and using them for His and man's benefit.

4) **"God saw everything that He had made, and behold, it was very good, suitable, pleasant and He approved it completely"** – God was satisfied with His creation of man; He approves of you because He created you and He is happy with His finished work in you.

GOOD - (ADJ.) - (BETTER, BEST)

- To be desired or approved of

- Having the required qualities; of a high standard

- Morally right; virtuous

SUITABLE - (ADJ.)

- Right or appropriate for a particular person, purpose, or situation

PLEASANT – (ADJ.)

⊛ Giving a sense of happy satisfaction or enjoyment.

⊛ Friendly and likeable.

APPROVE – (VERB)

⊛ (Often approve of) believe that someone or something is good or acceptable.

⊛ Officially acknowledge as satisfactory

God created you to have an intimate relationship with Him. God expects Man to look up to Him for approval, love and acceptance. God wants Man to: i) Call him Father- (Galatians 4:4 -7), ii) Be His son-God wants you to have a personal relationship with Him (Deut 7: 7-8 and 1 John 4:10) and iii) To share His Spirit - someone to feel His heart beat. God's desire is that you see Him as your Father in Heaven who is approachable at all times of the day.

God intended for Adam and Eve to remain in the Garden of Eden perpetually, fellowshipping and relating with Him but the serpent deceived Eve resulting in their exclusion from the Garden. Jesus Christ came as the last Adam to ransom fallen man back to God thereby reclaiming man's authority over satan. Jesus Christ gave us a new life, relationship and hope in God.

If you are still uncertain as to whether God has created you in His image for a purpose, I want you to know that He formed, sanctified, ordained and planned you for greatness before you began to show your presence in your mother's womb. This is confirmed in Psalm 139:16 which says *"Your eyes saw my unformed body; all the days ordained for me were written in your book before one of them came to be."(NIV).*

God definitely has a plan and purpose for your life that is bigger than anything expected by you, your family and friends.

Just because people do not believe in your dream or vision does not mean that it is not from God or that it would not happen as He has promised you. You must follow only God's plan and path for your life and not those of others because if you do, you will end up aborting God's purpose. God sanctified and ordained you for a particular assignment; you must align yourself to His calling for your life.

Now let us look at the definitions of the words "formed, sanctified, ordained, planned and Purpose" as taken from Your Dictionary.com:

FORMED – (NOUN)

- The shape, outline, or configuration of anything; structure as apart from colour, material, etc.

- The body or figure of a person or animal, a model of the human figure, esp. one used to display or fit clothes.

SANCTIFIED/SANCTIFY-

- To make holy; specif., to set apart as holy; consecrate, to make free from sin; purify,

- To make binding or inviolable by a religious sanction, to make productive of spiritual blessing

- Verb- deify, glorify, dedicate, consecrate

ORDINATION-

- Being ordained, as to the religious ministry,

- An installation,

- Consecration, coronation, investiture

PLAN (PLANNED) – (VERB)

- To plot an action in advance; prepare, scheme, devise, invent, outline, project, contrive, shape, design, map, plot, form a plan, think out, engineer, figure on, figure for, intrigue, conspire, frame, set guidelines, establish parameters,

- To have in mind – propose, think purpose; intend- (to destine for; design, mean, devote to, reserve, appoint, **purpose**, set apart, aim at, aim for, have in view).

PURPOSE – (NOUN)

- **Aim:** intention, end, goal, mission, objective, object, idea, design, hope, resolve, meaning, view, scope, desire, dream, expectation, ambition, intent, destination, direction, scheme, prospect, proposal, target, aspiration.

> *From the above definitions you can now understand that you were ordained by God from the beginning to be great, to have dominion and to rule without qualification or exception. The following points buttress this clearly:*

1. GOD PLANNED YOUR FUTURE BEFORE YOU WERE BORN -

"And Isaac prayed much to the Lord for his wife because she was unable to bear children; and the Lord granted his prayer, and Rebekah his wife became pregnant. [Two] children struggled together within her; and she said, If it is

so [that the Lord has heard our prayer], why am I like this?
And she went to inquire of the Lord. The Lord said to her,
[The founders of] two nations are in your womb, and the
separation of two peoples has begun in your body; the one
people shall be stronger than the other, and the elder shall
serve the younger" (Gen. 25: 21-23-Amp).

When Rebekah was having difficulty with her pregnancy, she enquired of the Lord who told her what plans He had for the children in her womb, He told her that she was carrying twins and that the older (Esau) would serve the younger (Jacob). God's promises never fail.

When Jacob grew up he received the inheritance God had ordained for him, although he deceived Esau to get it. Esau sold his Birthright to Jacob for bread and stew of lentils resulting in Jacob becoming the 'first-born' of Isaac as he had acquired the rights of the first born. Esau served his brother, Jacob for a time but he later broke Jacob's yoke from off his shoulder as prophesied by Isaac in Genesis Chapter 27. Jacob (Jews) forever remains more powerful and influential in the world today than Esau (Arabs) - See the books of Geneses, Obadiah and Malachi.

In Hebrews 12:15–16 we are told to exercise foresight and be on our guard always so that we do not lose the grace and blessings God bestows upon us as Esau did. Our prayer is that you would always hold onto your birthright in Jesus Name no matter was challenges come your way.

You might think you are insignificant or not equal to the next person standing by you but God has a far greater destiny for you than your peers or siblings. You must not look at where you are right now but to where God is taking you. When God calls you, He equips you for the journey ahead with His power and wisdom. God uses the foolish things of this world to confound the wise. You may not have been considered wise in human standards but when God finishes working on you, even the man of noble birth would not be able to match you in wisdom. God deliberately chose you when you were insignificant and lowly so that He can manifest His Glory through you.

Things will always work together for our good according to God's plans; design and purpose, for God loved us first and had predestined us from the beginning to be successful. The world would therefore have to make room for us to reach our destination. Ephesians 1: 4-5 says that God picked us for His own purpose before the foundations of the world. He foreordained us and planned us in love to be adopted as His children through Jesus Christ in accordance with His will and Intent. You must accept that you were made God's heritage and portion and you have an inheritance in Him. God works out everything in agreement with His counsel and design so that you will live to praise Him (Ephesians 1:11-12).

When God has ordained your success it will come to pass in fulfilment of His prophecy. God told Jeremiah that the plans He had for the children of Israel was to prosper them, to give them hope and an expected end, just as God told the Israelites then, He is telling us the same today (Jeremiah 29:11).

> "Then He said, Let Me go, for day is breaking. But [Jacob] said, I will not let You go unless You declare a blessing upon me. [The Man] asked him, What is your name? And [in shock of realization, whispering] he said, Jacob [supplanter, schemer, trickster, swindler]! And He said, Your name shall be called no more Jacob [supplanter], but Israel [contender with God]; for you have contended and have power with God and with men and have prevailed. Then Jacob asked Him, Tell me, I pray You, what [in contrast] is Your name? But He said, Why is it that you ask My name? And [the Angel of God declared] a blessing on [Jacob] there" (Gen. 32: 26-29-Amp).

God appeared to Jacob to let him know and understand that his location, position and placing in life were in His hands and that

His Word does not change. He made Jacob realise that his name change meant he was now able to walk in His calling and purpose.

1 Corinthians 2:9 states that eyes have not seen, ears have not heard and it has not yet entered into the heart of man, all that God has planned, prepared and proposed for those who love Him. You must, in faith, accept that the Lord has a greater plan for your life than where you are right now.

> *"For You did form my inward parts; You did knit me together in my mother's womb. I will confess and praise You for You are fearful and wonderful and for the awful wonder of my birth! Wonderful are Your works, and that my inner self knows right well. My frame was not hidden from You when I was being formed in secret [and] intricately and curiously wrought [as if embroidered with various colours] in the depths of the earth [a region of darkness and mystery]. Your eyes saw my unformed substance, and in Your book all the days [of my life] were written before ever they took shape, when as yet there was none of them. How precious and weighty also are Your thoughts to me, O God! How vast is the sum of them! " Psalm 139: 13-17 (Amp).*

King David praised God in Psalm 139 for forming his inward parts and knitting him together even when he was still in his mother's womb. He understood that God had designed his life in the darkness, before he had become a living being and that God had planned out the days of his life and written out his life in concrete. He knew that his ending would be far greater than his beginning because of God's hands upon his life.

Like David, God's plan for your life has already been written out in His Book before He formed you in your mother's womb. You were created to fulfil what was written of you in His Book. You therefore cannot go beyond or outside of God's Will or Ordination for your life. Anything else done would be acting outside His Will.

Your prayer should be "God please reveal all that you have written concerning me in your Book and help me to fulfil all you have ordained for me to accomplish". If you choose to ignore God's will thinking that you can fulfil your own purpose or programme in your own strength then you would fail. You should know that no one has the power to erase what God has written concerning you.

In Psalm 89:3-4; 20-27, King David reminded God of the covenant He had made with him which was unchangeable, unrelenting and irrevocable; I want you to know that God's promises are everlasting and perpetual. He does not change His mind but carries out His promises from one generation to the next, promoting generational blessings.

It is this same power of God residing within you that would enable you carry out His purpose for your life. You will do super abundantly, far over and above all that you could ever dare to imagine, ask or think. Because God has destined you to be above always; you will go far beyond your wildest imagination, thoughts and desires (Ephesians 3: 20). You must exalt and praise God for promising to do wonderful and marvellous things in your life.

2. GOD HAS GIVEN YOU AN ASSIGNMENT TO FULFIL -

You must discover what God's purpose for your life is and accomplish it. Your passion is a key to your assignment. You must realise that you are either sent on assignment by God or by the devil. You have to know where your assignment in life comes from. For those whose assignment emanates from God, their main goal will be to please Him in everything they do whilst those who have been assigned by the devil aim to wreck havoc in the lives of those they are sent to torment.

Your assignment is unique, special and distinct from others. Although Jeremiah, Elijah and Elisha had a wider platform, God also used Amos, Obadiah and Micah to reach their Nations.

God sent Jonah and Nahum to preach a message of repentance to the people of Nineveh; Micah was sent to the people of Samaria and Jerusalem whilst Obadiah was sent to the Edomites.

You must stay focused on your assignment and not allow envy, jealousy or covetousness make you run after another's. The discovery of your assignment will cause you to concentrate on the future instead of the past. **Your greatest achievement will be discovering who God has created you to be.** Your journey to discovery may be short or lengthy, it may take a few years or many years, it may be painful or hearty, no matter what it takes, discover who you have been designed, created and moulded to be in life and become that person.

Are you wondering what your God given assignment is? Your God given assignment is specific and unique to you. A clue to your assignment is a) your passion i.e. what you love doing, b) the problems you like to solve or c) what you hate and want to rectify. You cannot delegate your God given assignment to another to fulfil on your behalf. **Mike Murdoch** in his book entitled "*The Assignment*"[1] states that, "your assignment is not a decision…. It is a discovery. Your passion is God's gift to you; the problem you were designed to solve is your assignment."

When we were growing up we were often mocked by some people for helping those who they regarded as the "dejected, neglected and down trodden". We took offence because we did not understand that our passion for helping and assisting others was connected to our God given assignment. We now understand it was God who had placed those feelings and passions within us as children to prepare us for our future.

---

[1] The Assignment: Mike Murdoch

You must not allow other people's assignment to obstruct you from discovering who you are. Those who know that their assignment is from God do not fear the competition; they know that this earth is big enough for everyone's assignment to manifest. God has moulded you for greatness to become a person of value– priceless, irreplaceable and indispensable, live up to your calling.

If you feel that you are not fulfilling your life's purpose because you are not in full time ministry, we want you to know that you don't have to be a pastor, preacher or deacon before you can make an impact for God, start where you are today.

You may be a house wife/husband, know that your assignment is to your child or children that God has given you to nurture and to bring up in His way. Are you bringing your children up to know God for themselves? Don't think because you are at home all day long, you are not carrying out your assignment. Utilise the time at home to read study and pray so that you can become a better parent. It may be that God is using you to develop your children's gifts and talents so that he or she may become the next billionaire! Don't belittle your assignment.

You may be a nurse, doctor or carer, don't overlook your assignment. Do you realise that God is using your anointed hands to minister to the needs of the sick? Instead of complaining all day long, ask God to use you daily as a channel of divine healing to those you practice your profession on or care for.

You may be a clerical/ administrative worker; labourer or handy person; bus driver or road cleaner, think for a moment what would happen if you don't turn up for work? You may just find out that in your absence your employer can't function properly without you. God needs you to bring order to your employer's chaotic life, don't underestimate your importance!

You may be a business man or woman in the secular world and you feel that you are not fulfilling your assignment because you are at the heart of business, do you realise that you have the opportunity to sponsor the ministry with your finances?

The shepherds in Bethlehem who were grazing their sheep at the time Jesus Christ was born were assigned by God to announce His birth to the whole world. To some they were lowly mortals but to God they were priceless vessels who could be used for His purpose. He knew they would pass on His message as they saw it. They were the prefect candidates for the job (Luke 2:8-18).

Joseph and Mary were assigned by God to birth the destiny of Jesus Christ. They knew that their obedience to the call of God will alter the course of mankind so they yielded themselves to become instruments to be used by God. After Jesus Christ began His ministry, His parents took the back seat but without them just imagine what would have happened (Matthew 1:18-25, Luke 1:26-35).

God may have assigned you to others because He knows that you have a passion for seeing them delivered from their burdens, in helping them you learn more about yourself. Through others you discover what is needed to take you to the next level. Moses learnt too late that he had a temper and that God had assigned the stiff-necked people of Israel to teach him perseverance. You may have been assigned to people you don't want to take responsibility for because they are callous, unresponsive and hard. It is your responsibility to pray for God's guidance and strength to accomplish your assignment.

"So Moses said to the LORD, "Why have You afflicted Your servant? And why have I not found favour in Your sight, that You have laid the burden of all these people on me? Did I conceive all these people? Did I beget them, that You should say to me, 'Carry them in your bosom, as a guardian carries a nursing child,' to the land which You swore to their fathers? Where am I to get meat to give to all these people? For they weep all over me, saying, 'Give us meat, that we may eat.' I am not able to bear all these people alone,

*because the burden is too heavy for me. If You treat me like
this, please kill me here and now—if I have found favour
in Your sight—and do not let me see my wretchedness!"*
Numbers 11: 11-15.

Simon, the father of Alexander and Rufus, being on his way from the country passed through the path Jesus Christ took on His way to Calvary and was made to carry Jesus Christ's cross. Although some may say it was purely accidental or coincidental that Simon took that same path and was forced to carry the cross; we would say that it was divine providence (Mark 15: 21).

God might have ordained you to be a destiny enabler, don't overlook your role, as failure to carry out your assignment might have an everlasting consequence for you. Ask God to show you what He has in store for you. Joseph, the Arimathean was an honourable man who had purchased a tomb in a rock. He boldly presented himself to Pilate to take the body of Jesus Christ for burial. He later gave Jesus a dignified burial. When Joseph bought the tomb in a rock, he did not know that the place had been mapped out by God for the Rock of all Ages to be buried in it (*Mark 15:43-46*).

Your assignment is not mutually exclusive, whilst you might be assigned to others for a specific purpose, others might be assigned to you as well. You may be higher in position, it doesn't matter, humble yourself to receive help from those whom God has assigned to you. The Bible says that King David turned to the men of Issachar for help because they had an understanding of their times to know what David should do when he was threatened by Saul, he did not allow pride to hinder his blessing. You must decipher the spirit of those who have been assigned to you. Don't abort your own destiny by allowing pride to curtail you receiving help from others when you need it.

Don't determine a person's future by their present position or status; rather look at the assignment they carry within them. There are some people who have been assigned to you to be a ray of sunshine, don't overlook them; some may bring consistency and balance to your life whilst others may be painstakingly dedicated to you, don't ignore them.

Through the years we have been privileged to meet some wonderful people whom we are grateful to God for, we have learnt to appreciate and value them instead of being distracted by things that are immaterial and are of no significance. We have aunts, uncles and other family members who have been a blessing to us. They always step in when it matters the most, we are thankful to God for them.

There are people in your life who have the qualities you desire instead of being arrogant you should take the time to learn from them. You will always need people around you to uphold and strengthen you in times of trials and to rejoice with you in times of laughter.

God works everything together for the good of those who love Him. He knows how to manoeuvre things around and link us with those who will be a blessing to our lives. You must wait for God to work things out for you and not jump out ahead of God.

Aaron, Hur and Joshua followed Moses to the top of the hill when the Israelites fought against the Amelekites. When Moses became tired, Joshua and the two men held Moses hands up until he accomplished his assignment. You would always need others to assist you in fulfilling your assignment- you would need people who are spiritual warriors at heart to hold your hands up and stand in the gap for you.

> "Moses held up his hand, Israel prevailed; and when he lowered his hand, Amalek prevailed. But Moses' hands were heavy and grew weary. So [the other men] took a stone and put it under him and he sat on it. Then Aaron and Hur held up his hands, one on one side and one on the other side; so his hands were steady until the going down of the sun. And Joshua mowed down and disabled Amalek and his people with the sword"(Exodus 17: 11-13 Amp).

It is important for you to receive help in areas where you are weak or inadequate to ensure that they do not overshadow your strengths. Although Moses was spiritually focused on the tasks at hand he had overlooked the little things that eventually became important.

When Jesus was feeding the four thousand men and five thousand men respectively, He needed the help of his disciples to manage the crowd so that order could be maintained. If Jesus could seek the help of his protégés to fulfil His destiny then there is good reason for you to seek help from others.

3. GOD HAS ANOINTED YOU FOR GREATNESS TO MANIFEST HIS GLORY -

God has already anointed you for greatness so that you will live a victorious life and fulfil your destiny in line with His will. He has also anointed you to do great exploits for His Kingdom, so what are you waiting for? Psalms 8 states that God made man little lower than God Himself and He crowned man with glory and honour; that He also gave man dominion over all the Works of His Hands and that He put all things under his feet.

God's anointing is His divine enablement to accomplishing your assignment; don't waste the anointing on your life by being ignorant of its power. Do you realise that God's anointing on your life has qualified you to be the best candidate for the job? God has specifically equipped you to manifest His Glory in a unique way, if you pass the buck to someone else, they wouldn't shine. When you come to the realisation of whom God has created you to be, you will begin to walk in your ordination. Psalms 92:10 states that God has anointed you with fresh oil and has exalted your head above your peers, creation is therefore awaiting your manifestation, don't prolong the days. God has certainly endowed you with strength and has adorned you with the regalia of a king.

When the Spirit of the Lord comes upon you, your anointing will qualify you to do great and mighty things. Although Isaiah 61 bears reference to Jesus Christ, as Christians we should know that God has anointed us for greatness and He expects us to rise and shine so that His Glory can radiate through and within us.

Most people are short sighted or have limited understanding of the Power of God residing within them. You must discover what anointing God has placed within and upon you. You must ask God to reveal the hidden treasures within you because your ability to progress in life is dependent on your discovery of God's power residing within you.

You must accept that God, through the Gospel of Jesus Christ, has purchased you back from the Kingdom of satan and has redeemed you through salvation. He intends to use you as a symbol and a trophy for all to see and He intends to give you the treasures of the dark and hidden riches of the secret places.

God gave you a name before you knew Him or became aware of His presence. He did not call you to do nothing; He intends to bless you as a descendant of Abraham with a life of fruitfulness. There is not a creature that exists that is not known to God, God made each creature for a purpose and it is His Will that each creature manifests His glory in the form and manner that it was designed for, Psalms 19:1, states that "the heavens declared the glory of God and the skies proclaimed the work of His Hands," in the manner in which they were formed. As God has anointed you for greatness He expects you to proclaim your calling to the world in accordance with your anointing.

4. GOD WILL ENABLE YOU ACCOMPLISH YOUR PURPOSE DESPITE THE DOUBT OF OTHERS -

You were sanctified by God whilst you were in your mother's womb to fulfil your purpose in life and you will certainly accomplish that purpose. God will keep watch over His words to ensure that you become all that He has ordained and set you apart for. Your purpose may sound unbelievable to the undiscerning heart but with God no purpose is unattainable.

There are times when you tell others your dreams and aspirations and they laugh at or despise you because God has called you to do something so profound for them to understand, you must not at that time begin to retract the prophecy God has given to you or discard your dreams to please them. No matter how godly a person may appear to you, if they say things to you that do not align with God's purpose for your life you must silence them immediately. You must never abort your dream or abandon your assignment to please others (Mark 8: 27-33).

We know that God used someone like Othniel son of Kenaz, Caleb's younger brother to deliver Israel out of the hands of the kings of Mesopotamia whom Israel had served for eight years. He prevailed over Chushan-rishathaim and the people of Israel had rest for forty years. The fact that Caleb was used of God did not stop Othniel from shining.

God used Ehud, the son of Gera who was a left handed man to kill Eglon, King of Moab who had dominated the people of Israel for eighteen years; Ehud's victory resulted in Israel having rest for eighty years.

He used Jael, the wife of Heber the Kenite to obtain victory over Sisera, a general of Jabin's army, King of Canaan. She took a tent peg and a hammer in her hand and drove the pin into Sisera's temple, killing him instantly. God gave the glory of destroying the enemy into the hands of a woman, in her honour Deborah, a prophetess and Barak praised God for choosing Jael as His instrument of favour.

Jesus Christ made it known to those who opposed His vision that the very stone the builders had rejected had become the Chief Cornerstone. Whatever God has spoken concerning you will come to pass in due season. People may want to discriminate against you because they feel you don't qualify for the job but God does not consult others when He chooses to promote you. Sometimes it may be the other way round; we judge others because we don't understand what they are about.

> *God does not discriminate with people like men often do. He chooses and uses whom ever He pleases and whoever makes themselves available to Him.*

5. GOD EXPECTS YOU TO USE YOUR GIFTING IN HIS SERVICE -

God has anointed and filled you with wisdom, knowledge and understanding so that you can become effective in His Kingdom and on earth. He has given you specific and unique gifts, talents and abilities so that you can make Godly use of them for the benefit of the Kingdom. You must rise up to utilise the gifting on your life for His Glory. God has not endowed you with all these gifting, attributes and benefits only for you to remain idle in the House of the Lord or to use it for evil against others. Rise up and be counted amongst the saints as workers and vinedressers in the House of our God.

God anointed Bezalel, Aholiab and every wise man in Israel with divine insight, knowledge and understanding to build His Sanctuary and they made use of their gifting effectively. When Moses noticed their commitment and dedication he bestowed priestly blessing on them for the proper use of their gifts. When you understand God's specific and unique calling for your life, you will no longer waste your time doing the mundane rather you will focus on accomplishing your purpose. You have been created to excel and become a notable member of society; don't disappoint God who has invested so much in you by settling for the life of a mediocre.

6. GOD HAS EMPOWERED YOU TO POSSESS AND INHERIT THE NATIONS -

God created you to be a warrior and has given you a warrior's heart. A warrior never surrenders, quits or runs from the battlefront before the war is won. A champion never quits, he knows that failure births grounds for new strategy for overcoming; failure makes a champion change tactics to gain the ultimate and desired victory. God has already won the war on your behalf; your role is to go out and claim what your enemy has stored up for you.

> *It is God's intention that you inherit the nations and the uttermost parts of the earth as your possessions*

"I will proclaim the decree of the LORD: he said to me, "You are my Son; today I have become your Father. Ask of me, and I will make the nations your inheritance, the ends of the earth your possession" (Psalms 2: 7-8-NIV).

As God has promised that He will make the nations our inheritance and the earth our possessions, He expects us to go out and possess everything that belongs to us. He expects you to play your part in taking possession of your inheritance. You must not be idle because God wants to uplift your head high above your peers, contemporaries and enemies. You must remember that God has empowered you from the beginning to control your environment and to take possession of everything around you. When God entered into a covenant of blessing with Abraham, he swore by Himself since there was no one greater than Himself to swear by, to increase and multiply Abraham and to establish him in due season. God also makes these same promises to you, be assured therefore that your hope of prosperity and greatness will be fulfilled (Hebrew 6:13-20).

7. GOD HAS GIVEN YOU AUTHORITY TO COMMAND YOUR BLESSINGS INTO EXISTENCE -

God's desire is that you recognise and understand the authority that He placed inside of you. You must speak the word of God boldly and command into existence your blessings in faith, believing that your needs will be met by God according to His promises. You must not allow doubt, fear and unbelief to stifle your faith and keep God's promises from manifesting.

God has given you the authority to prophesy into your destiny and He will back up your words. He wants you to command your blessings into existence. It is God's will that whatever you forbid and declare to be unlawful and improper on earth would be forbidden in Heaven. So whatever you permit, allow or decree must be in consonance with what God has ordained or willed for you. Sometimes satan throws little white lies about the authority God has given to you at creation. You must remember that Jesus Christ has defeated satan indefinitely so that you can live a victorious life.

When you walk according to God's purpose, whatever you touch will be blessed, as He will cause rain to fall in its due season. You will not be afraid when you go out because God will be your everlasting shield. He will cause favour to overshadow your life as He Himself will confirm and ratify His covenant of blessings upon your life.

8. GOD WILL FIGHT YOUR BATTLES FOR YOU -

"He who vindicates me is near. Who then will bring charges against me? Let us face each other! Who is my accuser? Let

him confront me! It is the Sovereign LORD who helps me.
Who is he that will condemn me? They will all wear out like
a garment; the moths will eat them up" (Isaiah 50:8-9-NIV).

God intends to fight and conquer your enemies for you; put those who oppose you in His Hands and watch Him rise to smite them before you. Those who jeer at you in derision and contempt shall be brought low before you as God will not allow you to be put to shame. When the enemy comes against you like a flood, the Spirit of the Lord will put them in flight, your enemies will have no power to oppose your vision (Isaiah 59:19-NIV).

> *God's promises are rock solid and can never be broken no matter the alliance drawn against you to fight you.*

Balak, king of Moab sent the elders of Moab and Median to Balaam of Pethor to come and curse the people of Israel because he felt that they were too powerful for him, but Balaam could not do so because God was on their side. When Balak promised him more money and gifts; Balaam stated that even if Balak gave a house full of silver and gold, he could not go beyond the Word of God.

The Word of God is far reaching in our lives. God can take control of the vocal chords of those who oppose us and cause them to utter words of blessings over our lives. God will always reign supreme in our lives and no antagonist can alter that. No matter the alliance drawn up against us, God will rise and silence them on our behalf.

God permitted Balaam to go with the Princes of Moab because He intended to use Balaam to bless the people of Israel. Just as the Angel of the Lord stood with a sword as an adversary against Balaam so also will the Angel of the Lord stand up to protect us. He disappointed his benefactor by pronouncing God's blessings on

Israel which was pronounced on Abraham, Isaac and Jacob. When Balaam opened his mouth the negative words turned around and aligned itself with God's Word.

> *"Then the LORD met Balaam, and put a word in his mouth, and said, 'Go back to Balak, and thus you shall speak.' ... And Balak said to him, "What has the LORD spoken?" Then he took up his oracle and said: "Rise up, Balak, and hear! Listen to me, son of Zippor! "God is not a man, that He should lie, Nor a son of man, that He should repent. Has He said, and will He not do? Or has He spoken, and will He not make... He has blessed, and I cannot reverse it. "He has not observed iniquity in Jacob, nor has He seen wickedness in Israel...For there is no sorcery against Jacob, nor any divination against Israel. It now must be said of Jacob and of Israel, 'Oh, what God has done!' Look, a people rises like a lioness; and lifts itself up like a lion... Then Balak said to Balaam, "Neither curse them at all, nor bless them at all!" So Balaam answered and said to Balak, Did I not tell you, saying, 'All that the LORD speaks, that I must do?" (Numbers 23:16-26-NKJV).*

Not only did Balaam bless the people of Israel, he prophesied that Moab would be destroyed by a star that would come out of Israel. The curses that were intended for Israel were now imposed on Moab. He stated that out of Jacob shall come One who shall have dominion over the remnant of Moab. This prophecy refers to Jesus Christ who shall reign over all His enemies and shall have dominion over all those who oppose His kingdom.

God showed Jeremiah the plans his enemies had for him. God told Jeremiah that He would scatter their plots and bring them calamity for conspiring against him. All those who conspired against Jeremiah to abort his destiny had their own future aborted because they did not realise that the pit they were digging was meant for them (Jeremiah 11: 18-23).

God goes to the extent of warning your adversary to deal kindly with you. When Laban pursued after Jacob God warned him to lay his hands off Jacob because he carried the anointing for greatness. Since God has His Hands around you no one can frustrate your destiny (Genesis 31: 24- 29).

9. GOD INTENDS TO GO THE DISTANCE WITH YOU -

In Isaiah 46:3-4 God says that in your old age He will carry you because He has made you His responsibility. He will bear you up and save you from calamity. Sometimes you wonder whether God has forgotten you and all the promises He has made to you. Can a woman forget her nursing child? Would she not have compassion on the son of her womb! Although she may forget, God says that He will not forget you- He can never forget you because you are the apple of His eyes! (Isaiah 49:13-16).

God has imprinted you on His Hands and your face is continuously before Him. He cannot distance Himself from you because He has committed Himself to going the distance with you though it may appear that God has forsaken you, be rest assured that He hasn't.

CHAPTER 2

Obedience from those of the Past

(Old Testament - Patriarchs Who Walked According To God's intention for their lives)

There are many Patriarchs in the Old Testament who heeded the call of God for their lives and became pillars in their communities. Have you paid heed to God's holy call for your life? You can only fulfil your eternal purpose when you faithfully walk in the path that God has instructed you to take. Your dedication to God will never go unrewarded, as He will cause your light to shine before men.

You must not say to yourself that the level of obedience required by God from people of today is different from those who lived during the days of the Old Testament who were required to obey the Mosaic Law. God expects the same level of commitment and obedience from you as He did with those in the past.

Your continuing obedience to God will result in you fulfilling your destiny. Psalm 1:1-3-(Amp) says, *"BLESSED (HAPPY, fortunate, prosperous, and enviable) is the man who walks and lives not in the counsel of the ungodly [following their advice, their plans and purposes], nor stands [submissive and inactive] in the path where sinners walk, nor sits down [to relax and rest] where the scornful [and the mockers] gather. But his delight and desire are in the law of the Lord, and on His law (the precepts, the instructions, the teachings of God) he habitually meditates (ponders and studies) by day and by*

31

night. And he shall be like a tree firmly planted [and tended] by the streams of water, ready to bring forth its fruit in its season; its leaf also shall not fade or wither; and everything he does shall prosper [and come to maturity]"

When you remain firmly rooted in God and obey Him, He will remain in you, just as He did with the following Old Testament Patriarchs:

ENOCH

Enoch was a man of faith who walked habitually in fellowship with God all the days of his lengthy 365 years on earth. He was the son of Jared of Seth who was the third son of Adam and Eve. He was dedicated to God and lived up to his calling by following God's purpose for his life; his ways were pleasing to the Lord who rewarded him by taking him away so that he would not face death.

Enoch knew that God had made him in His own image and he lived in line with his ordination. His lifestyle and service to God was recorded as a testimony in remembrance of him. His name is included in the genealogy of Jesus Christ as Adams's offspring (Genesis 5:24).

NOAH

Noah, whose name means to rest, was given his name by his father, Lamech who believed that he would bring them rest and comfort from their labour on account of the ground being cursed by God. Noah was a righteous man who walked uprightly with God despite the spiritual apathy of the people around him who had forgotten their purpose on earth. God was saddened that He had given man dominion to rule over the earth as they had misused and abused their authority. Noah found favour with God because he obeyed and followed His instructions. God assigned Noah to build Him an ark according to the specifications given to him and Noah complied accordingly.

> *"I am going to bring floodwaters on the earth to destroy all*
> *life under the heavens, every creature that has the breath of*
> *life in it. Everything on earth will perish. But I will establish*
> *my covenant with you, and you will enter the ark—you*
> *and your sons and your wife and your sons' wives with you"*
> *(Genesis 6:17-18-NIV).*

After the flood God re-established His covenant with Noah and promised never again to curse the ground or to destroy man. He started anew with Noah and sanctioned him to become fruitful, to multiply and replenish the earth. God reinstated Noah with the dominion, power and authority, which Adam had lost in the Garden of Eden. God then set the rainbow as a token of His covenant between Himself and the Earth.

ABRAHAM

God called Abram and told him to gather himself and his immediate family to a place where He was sending them. In obedience Abram rose up and departed from the Land of Ur. Because Abram acted immediately on God's word, God compensated him by entering into an everlasting covenant with him to bless him, his descendants and posterity forever. God changed Abram's name to Abraham meaning "father of many nations" to confirm the covenant He had entered with him. God promised to distinguish Abraham amongst men and that there would be none in the East who would become as blessed as he was; Abraham received a new inheritance in God.

> *"NOW [in Haran] the Lord said to Abram, Go for yourself*
> *[for your own advantage] away from your country, from*
> *your relatives and your father's house, to the land that I will*
> *show you. And I will make of you a great nation, and I will*

bless you [with abundant increase of favours] and make your name famous and distinguished, and you will be a blessing [dispensing good to others]. And I will bless those who bless you [who confer prosperity or happiness upon you] and curse him who curses or uses insolent language toward you; in you will all the families and kindred of the earth be blessed [and by you they will bless themselves]" (Gen. 12: 1-3-Amp).

In response to God's faithfulness, Abraham built an altar to God to thank Him in advance for his coming blessings. It is imperative that at every stage of your journey you stop and thank God for His goodness and loving kindness towards you.

> *When you follow God's instructions He will cause you to prosper wherever you go.*

God promised to make Abraham's name great, to use him as an instrument of blessing to others and to make his seed as numerous as the stars. When you obey God's instructions He will make your name great amongst men. Your obedience will result in you prospering in whatever you do and wherever you go. You will find that what previously took you years to achieve will now only take a moment.

Although Abraham departed from his father's house, he took with him some of his relatives, notably Lot who later became a burden to him. You may have to jettison the excess baggage in your life if you want to arrive at your destination in life. For some of you it may be your friends, a habit, un-forgiveness, bitterness or a negative trait that is preventing you from fulfilling your purpose. Pray for the Holy Spirit's help to strengthen you so that you don't hang on to dead issues that will slow down your journey.

When Lot's herdsmen began to fight over resources with Abraham's herdsmen causing conflict in the tent, Abraham called Lot and told him that they should go separate ways to allow peace in their lives. Abraham realised too late that when God said he should leave his entire family, country and father's house, He meant just that. Lot parted ways with Abraham after he had chosen the Jordan Valley, which he believed was the most fertile part of the Land but God blessed Abraham by becoming his compensation and reward.

> *"The Lord said to Abram after Lot had left him, Lift up now your eyes and look from the place where you are, northward and southward and eastward and westward; For all the land which you see I will give to you and to your posterity forever. And I will make your descendants like the dust of the earth, so that if a man could count the dust of the earth, then could your descendants also be counted. Arise, walk through the land, the length of it and the breadth of it, for I will give it to you. Then Abram moved his tent and came and dwelt among the oaks or terebinths of Mamre, which are at Hebron, and built there an altar to the Lord" Genesis 13: 14-18-Amp).*

When Abraham became discouraged that God was prolonging the promises He had made to him concerning his wife Sarah, God reminded him that He is not a man to repent or change the promises that He had made to him.

> *"...God said to him, As for Me, behold, My covenant (solemn pledge) is with you, and you shall be the father of many nations.... And I will establish My covenant between Me and you and your descendants after you throughout their generations for an everlasting, solemn pledge, to be a God to you and to your posterity after you..." (Genesis 17: 3-10 Amp).*

As you are a child of Abraham by faith in God you are destined to become great by reason of the eternal covenant God pronounced on Abraham. The irrevocable and unconditional covenant between God and Abraham means that God's blessings will automatically flow to you and those around you whether you like it or not. God promised Abraham that He would bless whosoever blessed him and He would curse whosoever pronounced judgment or a curse upon him. The same covenant applies to you today, whosoever chooses to bless you God will Himself bless but whosoever chooses to have you as their enemy God Himself will become their enemy.

As Abraham was faithful, committed and dedicated to God, God honoured His Word to him and gave him a son whom he named Isaac. Abrahams' trust and faithfulness was accounted to him by God as righteousness (*Romans 4: 1-3*).

PHINEHAS

Phinehas, son of Eleazer, the grandson of Aaron changed the course of his own destiny because he stood up to the elders and chiefs of the people of Israel who had disobeyed God by joining themselves to Baal of Peor. After the people of Israel had settled in Shittim, they began to play the harlot with the daughters of Moab, which resulted in God's anger being kindled against them.

Whilst Moses was reprimanding the people involved in the open defiance of God's regulations and asking those not involved to kill the elders and chiefs who were involved in committing the act of idolatry, an Israelite man in defiance to Moses took a Midianite woman into his tent to have sexual intercourse with her. Phinehas in holy anger took a spear and thrust it through the Israelite man and Midianite woman causing the plaque, which God had set on the people to stop. For Phinehas' courageous act, God bestowed His covenant of peace on him and his descendants and He swore that the Priesthood would remain with his descendants forever (*Numbers 25:1-13*).

How do you respond when people stand against all that you believe in? Do you hide and hope that things will go away? Do you remain silent for fear of repercussions from the majority who may not be right? Or do you stand up for what is right? Your actions in times of conflict would show where your commitment lies. Phinehas did not sit on the fence or take the middle course but rather he was confrontational.

Phinehas was also instrumental in bringing peace to a volatile situation when the Children of Israel sent him as part of a delegation on a fact finding mission to the tribes of Reuben, Gad and half tribe of Manasseh. His character and temperament showed that he could be trusted to deal with delicate situations in a balanced manner (*Joshua 22: 30-33*). As a result of his commitment he found favour in God's sight.

JOSHUA

Joshua started out by being Moses' assistant and protégé. He knew the fulfilment of his destiny was tied to Moses who relied upon him to be faithful and loyal. He made it his duty to stay close to Moses no matter what came his way. His first assignment was to choose men to fight against the Amelekites; he complied with Moses' instructions and defeated the Amelekites.

He later followed Moses to the foot of the mountain to obtain the two tablets of stone, which contained the testimony and commandments of God. He distinguished himself and set himself apart from the crowd. He was steadfast in his service to God and did not depart from the temporary prayer tent when Moses went to speak to God face to face. He was chosen by Moses to be one of the twelve elders of Israel to spy out the land of Canaan. He was one of the two elders who brought back favourable report to Moses that Israel was able to claim Jericho as their inheritance. Due to his steadfastness, God told him that he would live to enter the Promised Land, as he was the minority voice that spoke out against the evil report of the other ten elders.

*"But Joshua the son of Nun and Caleb the son of Jephunneh,
who were among those who had spied out the land, tore
their clothes; and they spoke to all the congregation of the
children of Israel, saying: "The land we passed through to spy
out is an exceedingly good land. If the LORD delights in us,
then He will bring us into this land and give it to us, 'a land*

*which flows with milk and honey.' Only do not rebel against
the LORD, nor fear the people of the land, for they are our
bread; their protection has departed from them, and the
LORD is with us. Do not fear them." Numbers 14:6-9.*

When Moses knew that his time was up, he sought for a replacement; God told Moses to choose Joshua as his successor because God knew that Joshua was qualified to take over his mantle. He asked Moses and Eleazer to commission Joshua officially and to elevate Joshua in the presence of the Israelites.

God told Joshua that no man would be able to stand before him all the days of his life; he was told to be strong and courageous because God had a purpose for his life. God told Joshua to go on to accomplish the great tasks that were ahead of him. He reminded Joshua that the key to his success was obedience and focus.

*"Moses My servant is dead. Now therefore, arise, go over
this Jordan ...Every place that the sole of your foot will
tread upon I have given you, as I said to Moses. From the
wilderness and this Lebanon as far as the great river, the
River Euphrates, all the land of the Hittites, and to the Great
Sea toward the going down of the sun, shall be your territory.
No man shall be able to stand before you all the days of your
life; as I was with Moses, so I will be with you. I will not leave
you nor forsake you. Be strong and of good courage, for to
this people you shall divide as an inheritance the land which
I swore to their fathers to give them" Joshua 1: 2-6.*

Joshua did not relent in his effort at becoming the best leader, even in his old age Joshua continued to serve the Lord; he confidently confirmed that he and his household would serve the Lord.

CALEB

Caleb, the son of Jephunnah of the tribe of Judah was forty years old when he was sent with eleven other men to spy out the Land of

Canaan. He returned with a favourable report after spying out the land of Canaan. He told Israel to take possession of their inheritance for God was on their side; that God had given Canaan into their hands and they were able to accomplish everything God had ordained for them.

He showed what it meant to be an elder of his tribe, a man of valour and faith. He was confident that he could accomplish great things for the Lord; he had spiritual foresight and a discerning heart to understand what God was doing in the midst of the Israelites. He advised the people to disregard the ill report that his peers had brought back and to stop murmuring against Moses and Aaron. God took note of Caleb's attempts to soothe and comfort the people of Israel. He promised Caleb that he would outlive his antagonists; Caleb entered the Promised Land and was given a portion of the land as his inheritance.

> *"Then Caleb quieted the people before Moses, and said, "Let us go up at once and take possession, for we are well able to overcome it. But the men who had gone up with him said, "We are not able to go up against the people, for they are stronger than we." And they gave the children of Israel a bad report of the land which they had spied out, saying, "The land through which we have gone as spies is a land that devours its inhabitants, and all the people whom we saw in it are men of great stature. There we saw the giants (the descendants of Anak came from the giants); and we were like grasshoppers in our own sight, and so we were in their sight."*
> *Numbers 13: 30-33*

When Caleb was 85 years old he went to Joshua at Gilgal and reminded him of the promises God had spoken to Moses concerning him. Caleb said that he had been kept strong so that he could possess the land that God had promised him and that he was still ready to go to war on behalf of Israel to claim the promises of God. As a result of his boldness in asking, Joshua gave him the land of Hebron. Even after Caleb had claimed his inheritance, Caleb did not sit back rather he went out to defeat the three sons of Anak and the people of Debir. Caleb did not retire from active service as most of his contemporaries would have done but continued to serve the Lord faithfully (*Joshua 14: 6-15*).

You can learn from Caleb's life that it is never too late to start afresh or rekindle those desires locked within your heart. It is up to you to take a day at a time until you take hold of all that God has promised you.

GIDEON

Gideon was called by God to deliver the Israelites out of the hands of the Midianites. The Angel of the Lord appeared to Gideon whilst he was threshing wheat in the winepress and hiding from the Midianities, he was told that the Lord was with him and that he was a mighty man of valour. Gideon did not see himself as such because of his shortcomings, flaws and cowardice in standing up against the Midianites. He felt that he came from the weakest clan in Israel and that he was the least in his family.

When God decides to use you He will not look at your ethnicity or what position you hold in your family as He sees the wider picture and He has the end of the matter in sight. God knew that Gideon had the ability to become a mighty warrior even though he had not discovered it himself. God does not concern Himself with those who believe they are already on top of their game and un-bendable. God prefers to use those who are flexible, teachable and humble enough to follow His instructions.

> "And the Angel of the LORD appeared to him, and said to him,
> "The LORD is with you, you mighty man of valor!" Gideon
> said to Him, "O my lord, if the LORD is with us, why then
> has all this happened to us? And where are all His miracles,
> which our fathers told us about, saying, 'Did not the LORD

bring us up from Egypt?' But now the LORD has forsaken us
and delivered us into the hands of the Midianites." Then the
LORD turned to him and said, "Go in this might of yours, and
you shall save Israel from the hand of the Midianites. Have I
not sent you?" So he said to Him, "O my Lord, how can I save
Israel? Indeed my clan is the weakest in Manasseh, and I am
the least in my father's house." And the LORD said to him,
"Surely I will be with you, and you shall defeat the Midianites
as one man" Judges 6: 12- 16.

The Angel spoke into Gideon's future by calling him a courageous man who would do great exploits for God. God did not change His own perception of Gideon despite his inability to see himself as a mighty warrior. Despite the salutations, Gideon was not satisfied with the Angel's assurance so he asked for physical manifestations as evidence of God's approval.

After Gideon saw the signs, he went on to destroy the altar of Baal that his father had built. In the morning when the men of the city realised that Gideon had cut down their god they tried to kill him, but Joash, Gideon's father stood up for him. God also sent Gideon to destroy the Midianities and the Amalekities; He asked Gideon to reduce the number of his men from 32,000 to 300 so that when Gideon's army gained victory they would know that it was on account of God's favour. Gideon's army further destroyed Succoth and the tower of Penuel. God brought peace to Israel during the remaining days of Gideon's life (*Judges 6, 7*).

JEPHTHAH

Jephthah, the Gileadite was a mighty warrior but the son of a harlot; he was thrown out of his father's house and was disinherited by his brothers because he was considered an illegitimate child. He gathered around himself worthless men and fellow outcasts who he associated with.

When the Ammonites made war against Israel, his father's household sought him as they believed he met their requirements to represent their family to fight against their enemies. Although God had equipped Jephthah with the skills, talents and gifts that were necessary for his future, he had not put them to good use.

Jephthah was a wise and shrewd man who made his acceptance of going out to war conditional upon him being made the ruler over all the people. Not only did he rule over his household who had previously rejected him, but he ruled over the Tribe of Gilead and became the Commander in Chief of the army.

> *"And they said to Jephthah, Come and be our leader, that we may fight with the Ammonites. But Jephthah said to the elders of Gilead, Did you not hate me and drive me out of my father's house? Why have you come to me now when you are in trouble? And the elders of Gilead said to Jephthah, This is why we have turned to you now, that you may go with us and fight the Ammonites and be our head over all the citizens of Gilead. Jephthah said to the elders of Gilead, If you bring me home again to fight against the Ammonites and the Lord gives them over to me, [understand that] I will be your head. And the elders of Gilead said to Jephthah, The Lord is witness between us, if we do not do as you have said. So Jephthah went with the elders of Gilead, and the people made him head and leader over them. And Jephthah repeated all he had promised before the Lord at Mizpah"*
> *Judges 11: 6- 11 (Amp).*

Jephthah had initially utilised his skills for the wrong reasons, however when he had the opportunity to put them to good use in the service of God he rose to the occasion by going out to fight for his brethren. Our gifts would bring us to the forefront and make those who have ignored us take note of us (Judges 11:5-10). When Jephthah led the Israelites out to fight the Ammonites he vowed to sacrifice to God anything that first came out of his house if he gained victory over his enemies. On his return from war, his daughter came out to meet him. In anguish of heart he kept his covenant with God. He ruled Israel for six years.

SAMUEL

Samuel was a miracle child to his mother, Hannah who had been barren for many years. She gifted him back to God to minister in the Temple of God. His mother named him Samuel meaning "heard of God" or "God has heard". He ministered to the Lord at a time when the Word of The Lord was rare and precious like gold. The Word of God had ceased as Eli, the Prophet was no longer receiving any revelation from The Lord, and he had become luke-warm in his service to God. God chose Samuel to replace Eli as his successor as God saw that Samuel's heart was not polluted like those of Eli's sons whose actions had become abhorrent to Him.

> *"And the LORD called Samuel again the third time. So he arose and went to Eli, and said, "Here I am, for you did call me." Then Eli perceived that the LORD had called the boy. Therefore Eli said to Samuel, "Go, lie down; and it shall be, if He calls you, that you must say, 'Speak, LORD, for Your servant hears.'" So Samuel went and lay down in his place. Now the LORD came and stood and called as at other times, "Samuel! Samuel!" And Samuel answered, "Speak, for Your servant hears." Then the LORD said to Samuel: "Behold, I will do something in Israel at which both ears of everyone who hears it will tingle. In that day I will perform against Eli all that I have spoken concerning his house, from beginning to end" 1 Samuel 3: 8-12.*

Although Samuel knew that God had rejected Eli he still con-tinued to serve Eli faithfully until Eli's death. He turned Israel away from their idolatry and made them to serve God faithfully. When Israel went out to fight the Philistines in Mizpah, Samuel asked the people to put away their idols and sanctify themselves. He prayed and offered a sacrifice to the Lord on Israel's behalf and God caused Israel to have victory over their enemies. The hand of The Lord was against the Philistines all the days of Samuel's life.

When Samuel grew old, he made his sons Joel and Abijah Judges over Israel but they did not walk in God's ways. The Israelites rejected them and demanded a King over Israel. Samuel consulted the Lord who asked him to appoint Saul from the tribe of Benjamin as King. He became the King Maker who subsequently ordained the subsequent Kings of Israel. When Saul disobeyed God, Samuel was not afraid to rebuke him for his disobedience.

God instructed Samuel to anoint David whom he had over-looked as king over Israel as Saul's replacement. He made an error of judgement in looking at the external qualities of David's brothers instead of their internal attributes. God made it clear to Samuel that men looked on the outside but that He looked at the heart. Samuel was the last judge of Israel and he served God with all of his heart all the days of his life. He later died and was buried at Ramah and the children of Israel mourned for him (*1 Samuel chapters 1-25*).

JONATHAN, THE SON OF SAUL

Jonathan, the eldest son of King Saul was a faithful and loyal man who had a humble heart before God. God brought him to prominence when he showed courage by going with his armour bearer into the Philistines garrison to fight them as he knew God had granted the Israelites favour through him to defeat the Philistines.

On his return from victory he ate without knowing about the oath taken by his father. Saul wanted to kill him but was prevented from doing so by the Israelite army who stood up to defend him for his courageous victory over the Philistines. (*1 Samuel: 14*).

When Jonathan saw David being presented to Saul after the defeat of Goliath; he was so impressed with David's bravery and courage that his soul became knitted to David. Jonathan showed that he was not ashamed of forming solid ties with David. There is nothing wrong in forming solid relationships with people of the same gender, as their relationship has shown us.

"Now when he had finished speaking to Saul, the soul of Jonathan was knit to the soul of David, and Jonathan loved him as his own soul. Saul took him that day, and would not let him go home to his father's house anymore. Then Jonathan and David made a covenant, because he loved him as his own soul. And Jonathan took off the robe that was on him and gave it to David, with his armour, even to his sword and his bow and his belt" 1 Samuel 18:1-4.

Although they both came from different social backgrounds-Jonathan was the heir apparent whilst David reared sheep, it did not create a barrier to their relationship. Jonathan entered into covenant with David because he loved him as his own life. He stripped himself of his robe, which was on him and gave it to David; he also gave David his armour, sword, bow and girdle. By his actions he was telling David that he was vulnerable to him and trusted him with his life. There are many who knit themselves to others who become a yoke to them, you must always pray for discernment so that God would lead you to the right people to bare yourself to.

"And David stayed in strongholds in the wilderness, and remained in the mountains in the Wilderness of Ziph...Then Jonathan, Saul's son, arose and went to David in the woods and strengthened his hand in God. And he said to him, 'Do not fear, for the hand of Saul my father shall not find you. You shall be king over Israel, and I shall be next to you. Even my father Saul knows that.' So the two of them made a covenant before the LORD...and Jonathan went to his own house" 1 Samuel 23:14-18.

Jonathan showed himself to be of outstanding character, he chose to protect David from his father knowing that his actions would cause him to lose the throne and his inheritance. 1 Samuel 19: 1-7 and 1 Samuel: 20, records the length at which Jonathan went to protect David from his father. You are reminded of what true relationships are made off and the price you have to pay to preserve them.

As Jonathan noticed his father's negative and erratic attitude towards David he became concerned about David's wellbeing so he went down to strengthen and encourage David in the Wilderness of Ziph. He told David that when David became King over Israel, he would sit next to David. Jonathan deferred to David's vision as he recognised that God had positioned David to be king instead of his father. The act of allegiance sets Jonathan apart from many people who are solely interested in what they can obtain for themselves from a relationship. There is a lack of unity and support in many relationships where many want to be leaders instead of armour bearers. Jonathan showed himself to be a true armour bearer. He later met up with David to renew his covenant, it was the last time he saw David as he later died with his father and two brothers in battle.

When David heard of Jonathan's death, he gave a lamentation for him which can be seen in 2 Samuel 1:19-27. David knew that Jonathan was a mighty man and that his unconditional love radiated towards others he met.

ELIJAH

Elijah the Tishbite stood against Ahab and prophesied that there would be no dew or rain for three years and it happened as he had predicted. Although Elijah's servant did not see the rain coming, Elijah asked him to go and look out towards the sea seven times until his servant saw the revelation. Elijah provided for the widow in Zarephath and restored her son back to good health and life (*1 Kings 17*). He confronted Ahab and his followers for their worship of Baal, he gave the people one bull for the prophets of Baal and he took one bull for himself. He asked the false prophets to dress the bull and place it on their altar but must not put fire to it. He asked them to call on the name of their god whilst he called on the name of the Lord. He stated that the One who answered by fire, let Him be God. The false prophets cried to their god all day but nothing happened. When Elijah called upon the Lord later that evening God answered his prayer and sent fire from Heaven to consume the watered altar.

> *"Then Elijah said to all the people, "Come here to me." They came to him, and he repaired the altar of the LORD, which was in ruins… At the time of sacrifice, the prophet Elijah stepped forward and prayed: "O LORD, God of Abraham, Isaac and Israel, let it be known today that you are God in Israel and that I am your servant and have done all these things at your command. Answer me, O LORD, answer me, so these people will know that you, O LORD, are God, and that you are turning their hearts back again." Then the fire of the LORD fell and burned up the sacrifice, the wood, the stones and the soil, and also licked up the water in the trench. When all the people saw this, they fell prostrate and cried, "The LORD -he is God! The LORD -he is God!" 1 Kings 18: 30-39 (NIV).*

Elijah was so tuned in with God that God fulfilled all the words that proceeded out of his mouth. When Jezebel heard of what had happened and that Elijah had killed all her prophets, she wanted to kill him. He therefore fled from her presence and was preserved by the Lord. When Ahab and his wife, Queen Jezebel usurped Naboth's vineyard, Elijah confronted Ahab and denounced his throne prophesying that his kingdom would be torn out of his hands, Elijah then fled from Jezebel after prophesying doom upon her life. Shortly afterwards Ahab died in battle and King Jehu commanded that Jezebel be thrown out of the window.

As Elijah was confident in his gifting, he obeyed God by ordaining Elisha as his successor. He mentored Elisha who began to follow him everywhere he went until he was taken up in a whirlwind in a chariot of fire and never faced death (2 Kings). The Bible records that even after Elijah's death, his influence was still felt. He was regarded as John the Baptist and he is said to have appeared with Moses at Jesus Christ's transfiguration.

ELISHA

Elisha was picked by Elijah in an unusual manner to be his protégé and understudy. Elijah passed by Elisha, threw his mantle upon him, which caused Elisha to drop everything he was doing and follow him (Elijah) (1 Kings 19: 19-21). It is therefore not surprising that Elisha was ordained as his successor.

Elisha asked Elijah for a double portion of his anointing when he was departing. As Elisha had followed Elijah on his missionary journeys he was equipped to take over the mantle from him. He believed he had the right to request an uncommon blessing from his mentor. Although Elijah said it was a difficult request, he stated that he would grant Elisha's request on condition that Elisha saw him when he was being taken up at his departure. Elisha was alert to receiving his spiritual blessings; he stuck close to Elijah because he knew his master could be taken up at any moment. To ask for a double portion of Elijah's anointing could be considered greedy by some, but Elisha knew who he was and saw nothing wrong in asking to be doubly blessed.

> *"When they had crossed, Elijah said to Elisha, 'Tell me, what can I do for you before I am taken from you?' 'Let me inherit a double portion of your spirit,' Elisha replied. 'You have asked a difficult thing," Elijah said, 'yet if you see me when I am taken from you, it will be yours—otherwise not." As they were walking along and talking together, suddenly a chariot*

of fire and horses of fire appeared and separated the two of them, and Elijah went up to heaven in a whirlwind. Elisha saw this and cried out, 'My father! My father! The chariots and horsemen of Israel!' And Elisha saw him no more. Then he took hold of his own clothes and tore them apart. He picked up the cloak that had fallen from Elijah and went back and stood on the bank of the Jordan. Then he took the cloak that had fallen from him and struck the water with it. Where now is the LORD, the God of Elijah?' he asked. When he struck the water, it divided to the right and to the left, and he crossed over." (2 Kings 2: 9-14-NIV).

After Elijah's departure, Elisha became the leader of the Prophets. He parted the waters of Jordan and passed through it; he healed the water of the land that had caused miscarriage and barrenness and at Bethel he caused two bears to rip up forty-two boys who ridiculed him for being bald. In total he performed sixteen miracles and two resurrections of the dead.

He was concerned about the spiritual, financial, mental and emotional wellbeing of his people. He helped the widow of a prophet out of her financial indebtedness by asking her to collect vessels and to pour the little oil that she had into them, which resulted in the vessels filling up with oil. She was able to pay off her debts (2 Kings 4: 1-7). He rewarded the influential Shunammite woman who had provided for his comfort by prophesying that she and her husband would have a son within a year, as she had been barren for many years, his words came to pass. He later restored the woman's son back to life.

He further saved the young prophets' lives after they had eaten a deadly pot of soup; he also healed Naaman, the Commander of the army of the King of Syria from his leprosy by asking him to wash himself seven times in the River Jordan (*2 Kings 4, 5: 1-19*).

Elisha's life gives us an insight into what happens when you believe that God would come through for you during challenging times. When the King of Syria opposed Israel and went out to fight them, Elisha's servant cried out to him saying that the Israelite army would be defeated but Elisha prayed that his servant's eyes would be opened to see what was happening in the realm of the spirit, as the Hosts of Heaven had lined up to fight Israel's battle and they outnumbered the enemies of God.

When Elisha prophesied that the famine in the land would cease within twenty-four hours, the captain of the army on whom the king relied upon, said this could never happen. Elisha rebuked him and pronounced that he would see the miracle of abundance but would not partake of the blessings. The famine came to an end as predicted when the lepers at the City Gate found the booty in the Syrians camp.

Even after Elisha's death he still raised the dead, when a dead man's body, which was being carried for burial, was thrown into his grave and touched his bones, the dead man woke up (*2 Kings 13: 20-21*).

> *You must not shy away from asking God for double blessings of favour, financial wealth and spiritual anointing as Elisha did because a double anointing would cause you to do greater miracles than your peers, contemporaries and even your mentors.*

JOSIAH OF JUDAH

King Josiah was eight years old when he began his reign and he was not influenced by his fore fathers who had worshipped idols before him. In the 18th year of his reign, Hilkiah, the High Priest found the Book of the Law in the House of the Lord, Hilkiah gave it to Shapan, the Scribe who in turn gave it to King Josiah.

When King Josiah realised the consequences of Israel's indifference and idolatry in not following God's Word, he tore his clothes in humility. He sent Hilkiah, the priest to Huldah, the prophetess to seek God's face and petition God on behalf of his people. Prophetess Huldah prophesied disaster upon the inhabitants of Jerusalem and good tidings to King Josiah for honouring the Lord and repenting. The Bible records that there was no other king before or after King Josiah who turned to the Lord with all his heart, soul and might.

"Tell the king of Judah, who sent you to inquire of the LORD, 'This is what the LORD, the God of Israel, says concerning the words you heard: Because your heart was responsive and you humbled yourself before the LORD when you heard what I have spoken against this place and its people, that they would become accursed and laid waste, and because you tore your robes and wept in my presence, I have heard you, declares the LORD. Therefore I will gather you to your fathers, and you will be buried in peace. Your eyes will not see all the disaster I am going to bring on this place.' "So they took her answer back to the king" (2 Kings 22: 18-20-NIV).

King Josiah did not sit back after receiving this prophecy, but rather he continued in his zeal to serve the Lord wholeheartedly. He gathered his people together and read all the words of the Book of the Covenant, he slew also the altar priests and reinstated the Passover. King Josiah's purpose was predicted before his birth and he lived a life worthy of his calling.

"By the word of the LORD a man of God came from Judah to Bethel, as Jeroboam was standing by the altar to make an offering. He cried out against the altar by the word of the LORD: 'O altar, altar! This is what the LORD says: 'A son named Josiah will be born to the house of David. On you he will sacrifice the priests of the high places who now make offerings here, and human bones will be burned on you.'

That same day the man of God gave a sign: 'This is the sign
the LORD has declared: The altar will be split apart and the
ashes on it will be poured out" (1 Kings 13: 1-3-NIV).

King Josiah did right in the sight of the Lord all the days of his
life. He later died in battle when he rode out against the Egyptians.
On his death, Prophet Jeremiah gave a lament for him which was
made into an Ordinance in memory of his outstanding life; the
Lament is recorded in Lamentations 4:20- he was referred to as the
Anointed of the Lord. He was buried with honours according to
Prophet Huldah's prophecy in 2 Kings 22.

JOB

The Book of Job records the life of a man called Job. Job was said
to walk uprightly and blamelessly before the Lord because he
shunned evil from his life. He was regarded as the greatest man
from the East who got noticed by satan. The Lord asked satan if he
had considered Job, a man after His own heart, satan replied that
Job was only serving Him because He had hedged Himself around
Job, his family and possessions.

Satan was jealous of the relationship God had with Job that
he asked God to test Job's integrity and dedication to determine
whether Job would continue to serve God without the trappings
of his worldly possessions, family and health. God permitted
satan to test Job but told him not to touch Job's life (Job 1: 6-12).
In a single day, Job's children died, he lost his cattle, oxen and
worldly possessions, yet Job rose up, rent his clothes, shaved his
head and worshipped God because he understood that he had
come into the world with nothing and would depart this world
with nothing.

Satan was not content with Job's response so he asked God to
inflict Job with an illness to test his moral resilience. God gave him
permission to bring sickness upon Job but not to touch his life.

Although Job cursed the day that he was born, he did not curse God as satan had expected, even when Job's wife and three friends asked him to curse God, Job still refused to do so. Job believed God knew his end from the beginning and if God wanted to chastise him then he would endure the chastisement. He understood that his days had already been determined by God and that it was impossible for him to surpass the days allotted to him by God. Job said that even if God slew him he would still serve God. He realised that his suffering would pass in its due season and that unless permitted by God, satan had no power or authority over him (*Job 14*).

Job's family and friends believed that Job was being punished for his sins and that he was not humble enough to admit his suffering was a punishment from God. Although Job's friends had negative views and opinions of him, Job refused to adopt, justify or confirm their opinions to maintain their friendship.

In times of trouble satan would try to persuade you that others are the source of your problems, you must be alert to his devices. We must be cautious of concluding that a person going through trying times has sinned against God because God's way of testing people may be different from what we are accustomed to.

> *You must know who you are in Christ so that you don't allow others to distort your true perception of yourself.*

Job understood that bitterness could hinder his breakthrough, so he forgave his friends for their ignorance. God changed the captivity of Job around and restored his fortune and family to him. Job later had seven sons and three daughters; there was none who equalled his daughters in the East. Although Job's beginning was small, his latter days were greater than he could ever imagine. God wanted Job to know that He had far better plans for him, more than he could bargain for. Job's earlier success was nothing compared to his latter success.

> *"Now the LORD blessed the latter days of Job more than his beginning; for he had fourteen thousand sheep, six thousand camels, one thousand yoke of oxen, and one thousand female donkeys. He also had seven sons and three daughters... In all the land were found no women so beautiful as the daughters of Job; and their father gave them an inheritance among their brothers. After this Job lived one hundred and forty years, and saw his children and grandchildren for four generations. So Job died, old and full of days" Job 42: 12-17 (NKJV).*

Job's life is a testimony to us; we must expand our minds to fit into God's purpose for us. God's plan for our lives is greater than what we can ever imagine or think.

ISAIAH

Isaiah began his ministry on a low key; whenever he had a word from the Lord for his people he would take centre stage and deliver the message before retreating to the background. He spoke out against the social evils of his day and the contempt of the people in their worship of God.

When King Uzziah died, Prophet Isaiah saw a vision of who God was; he also discovered that he had not been operating in his full anointing. This revelation changed the course of Isaiah's life as he found new meaning and direction.

> *"Woe to me!" I cried. "I am ruined! For I am a man of unclean lips, and I live among a people of unclean lips, and my eyes have seen the King, the LORD Almighty." Then one of the seraphs flew to me with a live coal in his hand, which he*

had taken with tongs from the altar. With it he touched my
mouth and said, "See, this has touched your lips; your guilt is
taken away and your sin atoned for." Then I heard the voice
of the Lord saying, "Whom shall I send? And who will go for
us?" And I said, "Here am I. Send me!" (Isaiah 6:5-8-NIV).

Isaiah discovered that he was not as holy as he thought he was and that he had become lukewarm in his service of God. The Angel touched him to cleanse and sanctify him in preparation of his coming assignment. As a result of his new found commitment in serving God and running with God's purpose for his life, Isaiah became a notable prophet to be reckoned with. He saw the coming of Jesus Christ and the sign of the Virgin birth. He later became a symbol of sign and wonder to his generation (*Isaiah 7; 8 and 9*).

JEREMIAH

God sent Prophet Jeremiah to various Kings of Israel from the time of Josiah, King of Judah through to Zedekiah, until the captivity of Israel in Babylon. God told Jeremiah that He had ordained him for a special assignment before he had been formed in his mother's womb. God said he had sanctified, consecrated and set him apart as an instrument to reach the people of Israel and that he had been hallowed unto God, purposefully as a prophet to the nations.

"Then the word of the LORD came to me, saying: "Before I
formed you in the womb I knew you; Before you were born
I sanctified you; I ordained you a prophet to the nations."
Then said I: "Ah, Lord GOD! Behold, I cannot speak, for
I am a youth." But the LORD said to me: "Do not say, 'I
am a youth,' For you shall go to all to whom I send you,
And whatever I command you, you shall speak. Do not be
afraid of their faces, For I am with you to deliver you," says
the LORD. Then the LORD put forth His hand and touched

*my mouth, and the LORD said to me: "Behold, I have put
My words in your mouth. See, I have this day set you over
the nations and over the kingdoms, To root out and to
pull down, To destroy and to throw down, To build and to
plant." Moreover the word of the LORD came to me, saying,
"Jeremiah, what do you see?" And I said, "I see a branch of
an almond tree." Then the LORD said to me, "You have seen
well, for I am ready to perform My word" Jeremiah 1: 4-12.*

Like many of us, Jeremiah felt that he was not qualified to take on the mantle God had consecrated him for. He told God that he was not eloquent enough to speak before the people God had sent him to; God assured Jeremiah that He had already equipped him with the necessary skills and tools to fulfil his assignment.

When God calls you for a mission He knows that you are capable of carrying it out. Whatever you have been called to do, make sure you do it diligently. You might be shy or inarticulate and feel that you don't have the tools to pursue God's commission, just like Jeremiah you will succeed.

God told Jeremiah that his mouth had been touched so that when he opened it, he would speak that which he had been authorised, permitted and qualified to say. God knew Jeremiah was afraid of the people so He told him not to be afraid of their faces because He was with him (Jeremiah 1:17). God showed Jeremiah a branch of an almond tree, which signified His alertness and activeness in committing Himself to him. God made Jeremiah strong and bold to withstand those who would oppose him, He commissioned Jeremiah to become a watchtower to his people to warn them about their attitude towards God.

God opened Jeremiah's spiritual eyes to see the plans of his enemies who had gathered themselves against him to cut his assignment short. He frustrated their schemes so that their plans failed against Jeremiah. God showed Jeremiah the resentment his household had towards him because they were embarrassed by his calling. God would be a shield around you to protect you from impending dangers and He will frustrate the plans of your enemies who seek to halt your journey (*Jeremiah 11; 12*).

God tested Jeremiah's faithfulness by asking him to do foolish things for Him. Although Jeremiah complained about his ridicule, God told him that he would be rewarded by having his life spared whilst in captivity. When Jeremiah was thrown in prison by Pashhur and he became a laughing stock to those who met him, he found favour with Ahikam, son of Shaphan who did not allow the people to kill him.

> *God knows the plans and thoughts He has towards you, they are certainly not for evil but to give you a good and expected end (Jeremiah 29:11).*

God says He is the God of all flesh and that there is nothing too hard for Him to do in your life. You must believe that His plans for your life would come to pass. Call upon God who will answer you and show you great and mighty things that He has planned for you. God planned your future before you were even conceived and before you were moulded together to become a living being. God sanctified and consecrated you before the foundations of the world so that you will rise up to the challenges of your ordination and fulfil His purpose for your life.

What legacy do you want to leave behind after you have gone? If you want your family or generation to rise up and call you blessed, then you must fulfil your destiny. Creation is waiting for you to manifest all that God has stored inside of you, don't disappoint Him.

EZEKIEL: THE SON OF BUZI

Prophet Ezekiel was taken into exile to Babylon where he lived amongst his fellow Jews. Whilst in captivity seated by the river Chedbar in Babylon, he saw a vision from the Lord that changed the course of his life. He saw God present a scroll to him to eat in preparation of his assignment (*Ezekiel 2*).

> *"Then He said to me: "Son of man, go to the house of Israel and speak with My words to them. For you are not sent to a people of unfamiliar speech and of hard language, but to the house of Israel, not to many people of unfamiliar speech and of hard language, whose words you cannot understand. Surely, had I sent you to them, they would have listened to you… Behold, I have made your face strong against their faces, and your forehead strong against their foreheads… Like adamant stone, harder than flint, I have made your forehead; do not be afraid of them, nor be dismayed at their looks, though they are a rebellious house." Moreover He said to me: "Son of man, receive into your heart all My words that I speak to you, and hear with your ears. And go, get to the captives, to the children of your people, and speak to them and tell them, 'Thus says the Lord GOD,' whether they hear, or whether they refuse." …Now it came to pass at the end of seven days that the word of the LORD came to me, saying, "Son of man, I have made you a watchman for the house of Israel; therefore hear a word from My mouth, and give them warning from Me:" Ezekiel 3: 4-17*

God told Ezekiel that He was equipping him for the journey ahead and He filled Ezekiel's heart with the words that he would utter in the future. He made Ezekiel a watchman to the House of Israel to invite them to repent of their evil ways before it was too late. He also told Ezekiel to prophesy against the false prophets who had been deceiving the people of Israel (*Ezekiel 4*).

Ezekiel saw things that were hidden from the natural eyes. He saw the true hearts of the seventy elders of Israel who were worshipping idols in secret; he saw the women who were weeping and worshipping Tammuz in the north gate of the Lord's house, and the twenty-five men who had their faces turned towards the east, bowing down to worship the sun (*Ezekiel 8-9*).

God also showed Ezekiel the twenty-five men who had been devising iniquity and giving wicked counsel against Israel. These elders of Israel should have been praying for the restoration of Israel yet they were plotting her downfall so that they could benefit from her failure. Whilst Ezekiel was prophesying against their evil plans, Peletiah, one of these elders died (Ezekiel 11).

The Lord told Ezekiel that He knew the things that came into the hearts of men and He could not be deceived. When some of the elders of Israel came to Ezekiel to enquire of the Lord, God revealed their hearts to him. When you are in consonance with God, you will discern the hearts of those around you (*Ezekiel 11*).

God set up Ezekiel in the valley, which was full of dry bones and asked him whether these bones could live again, Ezekiel replied that it was only God who knew. God gave him the power to command breath and spirit to enter into the bones so that they could be resurrected. Ezekiel prophesied and saw what was impossible happen (*Ezekiel 37:1-14*). He saw the spirit of life, the spirit of God, enter into the dead bones and they became alive.

As a believer no matter how DEAD your dreams and aspirations appear to be, with God in the equation everything is possible. Your doctor may have told you that it is not possible to have that child or to be healed of that sickness and/or your financial consultant may tell you there is no way out of your financial crisis, I want you to know that God will open your grave and cause you to come out of your dire situation; He will cause a turn around for you.

In Ezekiel's 25th year, he was set upon a very high mountain where he saw a vision of hope. You too must rise up higher to a new dimension in order to see what surrounds you so that you can live victoriously.

AMOS

Amos, a herdsman in Tekoa was called by God to admonish the noble members of the society who had discarded God from their lives. These Nobles had allowed their financial success to draw them away from God. He called his people to true repentance and asked them not to perform outward acts of repentance that did not come from their hearts. He warned Judah and Israel that despite being chosen and set apart by God, God would spew them out of His mouth at any time because of their arrogance and presumptuous attitude that God could not forsake them (*Amos 2, 3*).

Amaziah, the prophet of Bethel gave a bad report to king Jeroboam about Amos, He also told Amos to stop preaching. Amos responded by telling Amaziah that it was God and not man who had called him to speak to the people of Israel, so he would not remain silent. Amos cursed Amaziah for his folly in trying to silence the Prophet of God.

Amaziah equally told Amos to leave the city where the king's palace was and to retire into obscurity. He forgot that God had to be involved in the king's governance for his reign to be established. Amaziah believed that Amos was meant to preach to only the poor who needed religion. He forgot that if the rich amongst them were to retain their wealth they needed God to direct their path.

"Then Amaziah said to Amos, "Get out, you seer! Go back to the land of Judah. Earn your bread there and do your prophesying there. Don't prophesy anymore at Bethel, because this is the king's sanctuary and the temple of the kingdom." Amos answered Amaziah, "I was neither a prophet nor a prophet's son, but I was a shepherd, and I also took

care of sycamore-fig trees. But the LORD took me from tending the flock and said to me, 'Go, prophesy to my people Israel. 'Now then, hear the word of the LORD. You say, 'Do not prophesy against Israel, and stop preaching against the house of Isaac.' "Therefore this is what the LORD says: 'Your wife will become a prostitute in the city, and your sons and daughters will fall by the sword. Your land will be measured and divided up, and you yourself will die in a pagan country. And Israel will certainly go into exile, away from their native land" Amos 7:12-17.

You must not allow others to sabotage the dreams that God has placed in your spirit. You must not allow anyone to cancel, nullify or weaken your dream. God who has called you has qualified you to take on the city people, royalty and nobility so you must rise to the occasion. Do not allow people to intimidate you to silence. Although Amos was a shepherd by profession; God had called him to be a shepherd of His people. Never give in to people's demands to retire into obscurity.

OBADIAH

Obadiah, a chief in King Ahab's household was used by God to hide one hundred prophets in a cave when Queen Jezebel sought to kill them. Prophet Elijah sent Obadiah to King Ahab to tell him to meet him at an arranged place and time. (1 Kings 18: 4). God sent Obadiah to speak against the Edomites, the descendants of Esau who had elevated themselves in their own eyes.

He prophesied that God would bring them down from their lofty place and punish them for the sins of their forefathers who had refused to assist the Israelites when they sought their help. The Edomites had joined forces with Israel's enemies to plunder Israel (Book of Obadiah). Although Obadiah was a minor prophet, he was still effective in his service of God.

JONAH

God sent Jonah, son of Amittai to Nineveh to preach a message of repentance to them as He intended to punish Nineveh for their sins; however Jonah was reluctant to go to Nineveh so he fled and went along to Joppa to board a ship to Tarshish.

God did not disregard Jonah's disobedience; He punished Jonah by causing a storm on the seas so that the ship became distressed. When the sailors and owners of the ship called to their gods for help nothing happened, so they woke Jonah from his sleep to pray to his God. They casted lots, which fell on Jonah; he admitted that the storm was caused by God because of his refusal to carry out God's assignment.

The captain later threw Jonah over board to distil the tempest. He landed straight into the mouth of a big fish that God had sent to preserve his life. Jonah was upset that God had nominated him to preach to the people of Nineveh because he knew that God would forgive them if they repented. Jonah believed that salvation should be earned from God and not bestowed graciously on the undeserving by God.

God later permitted the fish to vomit Jonah on dry ground after three days and told Jonah to proceed to his assignment. After Jonah preached to the people of Nineveh, the king, his nobles and subjects fasted and prayed to God who forgave them. However, instead of Jonah rejoicing he became angry again with God and began to sulk. He asked God to kill him and he went out of the city to sit and whinge. God provided a shade for Jonah to recuperate, instead of rebuking and punishing him.

"But Jonah was greatly displeased and became angry. He prayed to the LORD, "O LORD, is this not what I said when I was still at home? That is why I was so quick to flee to Tarshish. I knew that you are a gracious and compassionate God, slow to anger and abounding in love, a God who relents

from sending calamity. Now, O LORD, take away my life, for
it is better for me to die than to live." But the LORD replied,
"Have you any right to be angry?" (Jonah 4: 1-4-NIV).

God calls us at different stages of our spiritual journey so He knows our level of maturity. Rather than punish us, He would sometimes wrap His Hands around us and scold us gently for our childish tantrums. God bestows upon us unmerited favour and love so that we can become all that He had destined us to be.

Although Jonah initially disobeyed God, he later complied with God's instructions. Jonah's evangelistic mission to Nineveh was successful and he learnt that man was more valuable to God than possessions (Book of Jonah). When you run away from God's assignment be rest assured that He would find you out to ensure that you obey His instructions. The Psalmist says:

"Where can I go from Your Spirit? Or where can I flee from
Your presence? If I ascend into heaven, You are there; If I
make my bed in hell, behold, You are there. If I take the
wings of the morning, And dwell in the uttermost parts of
the sea, Even there Your hand shall lead me, And Your right
hand shall hold me." Psalms 139: 7-10

You must not fail to heed God's calling on your life, if you refuse to carry out the simple instructions He gives you, He would readily look for another willing person to take your place. We pray that this would never be your portion in Jesus' name.

HAGGAI

Prophet Haggai ministered in the days of King Darius of Babylon. God assured him that the latter glory of His House would be greater that the former days. God sent Haggai to tell Zerubabel that He intended to fulfil the covenant He had made concerning Israel. Zerubbabel at that time felt disillusioned that God's temple was not being re-built and his enemies were delaying the building of God's Temple.

Haggai challenged his people to serve God faithfully and to return back to Him wholeheartedly. He encouraged Zerubbabel and the returnee exiles that there was nothing impossible for God to do. He encouraged them to trust in God who would meet all their needs in His own time.

> "Speak to Zerubbabel… Ask them, 'Who of you is left who saw this house in its former glory? How does it look to you now? Does it not seem to you like nothing? But now be strong, O Zerubbabel,' declares the LORD. 'Be strong, O Joshua son of Jehozadak, the high priest. Be strong, all you people of the land,' declares the LORD, 'and work. For I am with you,' declares the LORD Almighty. 'This is what I covenanted with you when you came out of Egypt. And my Spirit remains among you. Do not fear.' … 'The silver is mine and the gold is mine,' declares the LORD Almighty. 'The glory of this present house will be greater than the glory of the former house,' says the LORD Almighty 'And in this place I will grant peace,' declares the LORD Almighty" (Haggai 2:2-9-NIV).

This prophecy applies to your life too; your former glory, success and achievements will be nothing compared with the future glory that is coming your way. You have not left the "world" to serve God in vain. He says you should not fear because in a short while you would see His Mighty Hands upon you. God will shake the nations for your sake and will fill your house with His Glory.

ZECHARIAH

Prophet Zechariah preached during the time of King Darius. He also had a word from God for Zerubbabel that it was neither by his might nor by his physical strength but by God's power that victory will come. God had ordained Zerubbabel to go forth from captivity to rebuild the Temple of God but his enemies had tried to hamper his assignment. God promised Zerubbabel that as his hands had laid the foundations of His Temple; his same hands will finish it.

> "So he said to me, "This is the word of the LORD to Zerubbabel: 'Not by might nor by power, but by my Spirit,' says the LORD Almighty. "What are you, O mighty mountain? Before Zerubbabel you will become level ground. Then he will bring out the capstone to shouts of 'God bless it! God bless it!' "Then the word of the LORD came to me: "The hands of Zerubbabel have laid the foundation of this temple; his hands will also complete it. Then you will know that the LORD Almighty has sent me to you. "Who despises the day of small things? Men will rejoice when they see the plumb line in the hand of Zerubbabel. "(These seven are the eyes of the LORD, which range throughout the earth.)"
> Zechariah 4:6-10 (NIV).

There will be no mountain, valley or highway that will be able to stop what God has destined for you.

God laid the foundations of your life, He moulded you and sent you forth to accomplish purpose- by the Grace of God you will accomplish your purpose! God asked who despises the days of small beginnings, don't look at where you are today, a time is coming when people will want to know you and to be associated with you. In Zechariah 8: 23 God told Zechariah to tell the people of Israel that a time is coming when men from every nation will take hold of the hem of their robe and say let us go with you because we have heard that your God is with you, this will be your portion in Jesus' Name.

MALACHI

Prophet Malachi gave the last word in the Old Testament, he reminded Israel of the love God had for Jacob by choosing him above Esau his brother. God has shown this same love to us by choosing us as His instruments to manifest His glory. He chose Israel to be called by His Name so that they could honour, love and worship Him.

Malachi spoke to Israel about their spiritual indifference to God and called them to true repentance. He said that God was displeased with the manner of their worship of Him; that He abhorred the sacrifices they brought to Him; that He could no longer tolerate their attitude towards Him; that the priests had failed in their spiritual obligations to the people and that they had disregarded the sanctity of marriage. Malachi told them that when they truly repented of their sins God would return to them.

We must worship and honour God wholeheartedly if we are to succeed in everything we do. When God is satisfied with our worship and praise, He will fulfil His part of the bargain and open the floodgates of Heaven to bless us with an everlasting blessing that will ripple down to our descendants.

The Old Testament closes with promises of a better future making way for a New Covenant. The old failures in your life will pass away to make room for your coming blessings (Book of Malachi).

You may have observed that the people mentioned in this Chapter had different abilities and temperaments but God still used them to get His work done. Just like these people God too will use your own individual ability and temperament for His kingdom. All He requires of you is that you are a willing and obedient steward.

CHAPTER 3

Walking in a New Covenant

(New Testament - Persons Who Walked According to God's Purpose for Their Lives)

You are called according to God's purpose, to show forth His Majesty and His marvellous works. Jesus Christ created a new covenant between God and His people. You must walk in this new covenant that Jesus Christ has purchased you into. Jesus Christ came to give us hope, a future and an expected end. Creation is awaiting your manifestation, therefore walk uprightly in your calling.

The Holy Spirit has given us the power to share in the inheritance of Jesus Christ and to enjoy fellowship with God, which God had intended before Man's fall. We are now guaranteed eternal life in Christ through our salvation. Jesus Christ purchased eternal life for us through the shedding of His Blood at Calvary. Although eternal life in this new covenant with Christ is free, you must remain attached to Him.

The New Testament records examples of men and women who heeded the call of God for their lives; they were obedient to God and utilised their anointing and gifting for the benefit of the church. Amongst these are:-

JOHN THE BAPTIST

John the Baptist was born to Zechariah and Elizabeth who had awaited his birth for years. He was a destiny child who came to fulfil the prophecy given in the Old Testament.

> *"Behold, I will send you Elijah the prophet before the great*
> *and terrible day of the Lord comes. And he shall turn and*
> *reconcile the hearts of the [estranged] fathers to the [ungodly]*
> *children, and the hearts of the [rebellious] children to [the*
> *piety of] their fathers [a reconciliation produced by repentance*
> *of the ungodly], lest I come and smite the land with a curse*
> *and a ban of utter destruction". Malachi 4:5-6 (Amp).*

Luke, Chapter 1 records that during John the Baptist's circumcision on the eight day it was evident to all that he was born for a particular purpose; the people recognized that he carried a great mantle on his life. John was different from his contemporaries, he was direct and assertive as he told the people of Judea to change and repent of their sins. He knew that he had a short time to carry out his assignment on earth and therefore he began his ministry in earnest as a forerunner of Jesus Christ.

> *'Truly I tell you, among those born of women there has*
> *not risen anyone greater than John the Baptist; yet he who*
> *is least in the kingdom of heaven is greater than he. And*
> *from the days of John the Baptist until the present time,*
> *the kingdom of heaven has endured violent assault, and*
> *violent men seize it by force [as a precious prize—a share*
> *in the heavenly kingdom is sought with most ardent zeal*
> *and intense exertion]. For all the Prophets and the Law*
> *prophesied up until John. And if you are willing to receive*
> *and accept it, John himself is Elijah who was to come [before*
> *the kingdom]" (Matthew 11: 11-14 Amp).*

John knew his purpose in life and followed it; he did not seek to copy others but concentrated on his own calling. He initially protested when Jesus Christ came to him to be baptised in the Jordan but when Jesus Christ reminded him of his role as a fore-runner, he complied.

As a result of John's obedience, he saw the Heavens open and the Spirit of God descend like a dove on Jesus Christ. It was John's duty to fulfil righteousness by leading the way for the One who was coming to reconcile the hearts of the lost to God (*Luke 1: 16-17*).

Whilst John was in prison, he heard about the miracles being performed by Jesus Christ so he sent two of his disciples to Jesus to enquire whether He was indeed the One spoken about in the scriptures. John was not content with hearsay evidence; he wanted to establish for himself whether Jesus Christ was the One he had been preparing the ground for. He knew that his time would shortly be up so he wanted to satisfy himself that he had fulfilled God's assignment for his life. Jesus Christ sent a response to John that he was not mistaken about his belief (*Luke 7: 17-28*). He was later killed because he spoke the truth without compromising the Word of God.

JESUS CHRIST

When Mary became pregnant through the Holy Spirit she was told about God's purpose for her baby. She was told that her son shall be called Jesus, the Saviour of mankind and that He was to reconcile man back to God. Jesus Christ was better equipped to put Himself forward to sacrifice Himself for the restoration and redemption of man. Luke records in Chapters 1: 30-33 that Jesus Christ's purpose had been pre-determined by God before He was born.

The wise men from the East recognised that Jesus Christ was born for a purpose. They knew the meaning of His star and realised that they had stumbled on something so great and profound that they had to find out what it meant. They travelled far to seek the child so that they could pay homage to Him.

"NOW WHEN Jesus was born in Bethlehem of Judea in the days of Herod the king, behold, wise men [astrologers] from the east came to Jerusalem, asking, Where is He Who has been born King of the Jews? For we have seen His star in the east at its rising and have come to worship Him" (Matthew 2:1-2-Amp).

Jesus was tempted at the beginning of his ministry by satan who sought to distract Him from His calling. Jesus being secure in His own identity and knowing what power resided within Him told satan to get behind Him. satan told Jesus that he would give Him power and dominion if Jesus were to prostrate Himself before him and pay him homage. Jesus rightly told satan to get behind Him (*Matthew 4: 3-11*).

When you are aware of God's authority in your life and recognize that your identity comes from God you will not bow to adversity, any contrary wind or to the devil. The result of walking in the authority that you have in Christ will be evident, as you will stand apart from others.

Although Jesus preached to multitudes of people, He never lost focus of what God's purpose was for His life. At each stage, He took His disciples aside to rest and pray. He rested so that He could be strengthened to carry out His assignment and He prayed so that He could hear from God.

Jesus Christ revealed His calling to others. On one Sabbath, He entered the Synagogue in His hometown to let His people know that God had a purpose for Him to fulfil. He opened the Scroll and read from the book of Isaiah 61 in the hearing of those present that He had come to fulfil scripture. He wanted them to know that He had spent the last thirty years preparing for His public ministry and He intended to accomplish His purpose. *Isaiah 61:1-3 (Amp) says, "THE SPIRIT of the Lord God is upon me, because the Lord has anointed and qualified me to preach the Gospel of good tidings to the meek, the poor, and afflicted; He has sent me to bind up and heal the broken hearted, to proclaim liberty to the [physical and spiritual] captives and the opening of the prison and of the eyes to those who are bound, To proclaim the acceptable year of the Lord [the year of His favour] and the day of vengeance of our God, to comfort all who mourn, To grant [consolation and joy] to those who mourn in Zion— to give them an ornament (a garland or diadem) of beauty instead of ashes, the oil of joy instead of mourning, the garment [expressive] of praise instead of a heavy, burdened, and failing spirit—that they may be called oaks of righteousness [lofty, strong, and magnificent, distinguished for uprightness, justice, and right standing with God], the planting of the Lord, that He may be glorified."*

Jesus could have abandoned His goal to die for mankind in order to be accepted by the crowd but He chose not to do so. The decision to obey God and run with the vision He has given to us depends on each of us; we must always consider the wider picture as our disobedience may have an adverse effect on others.

When Jesus was expounding the scriptures in a temple in Galilee, the Jews that were present were astonished at His level of comprehension. Jesus told them that His ability came from God who had ordained Him to speak with such authority. He said that His wisdom and teaching came from the Throne of God and that after His glorification they would recognize who He is.

What do you do when you are challenged by others? Do you abandon your destiny to please them or do you run ahead with the vision God has given you and remain true to your convictions? You must take responsibility in making the world know what your purpose in life is, if you don't, God would have to look for others to accomplish His purpose for mankind. When you align yourself to God's will, He will order your footsteps and automatically give you the wisdom, knowledge and skills required to fulfil your purpose.

Jesus Christ performed about thirty-seven miracles; He healed the sick, resurrected the dead and strengthened the faith of His disciples and followers. He wanted the world to know who He was, what He stood for and who had sent Him. He wanted people to trust in Him as their source and strength. He declared that He is the Truth, The Life, and The Way; that no one can get to the Father- God except through Him. He is our Light and Shining Armour, the "I Am" of our life and the Ancient of Days.

On account of Jesus Christ's obedience in sacrificing Himself on the cross, the centurion that stood by acknowledged that Jesus Christ was truly the Son of God and he gave his life to God that day. Jesus Christ told Nicodemus, a teacher of the Law that His purpose was to die for mankind so that everyone who believes in Him would not perish but have eternal life (*John 3*).

This is now an opportunity for you to give your life to Jesus Christ or to rededicate your life to Him as He is standing at the door of your heart knocking to be let into it. He guarantees you eternal life from this time onwards. He says that He would not cast away anyone who seeks Him.

John 3:16 says "that for God so loved the world, that He gave His begotten Son, that whomsoever believes in Him will not perish but have everlasting life".

Ephesians 2: 8-10 says, "For by grace you have been saved through faith and that not of yourselves; it is the gift of God, not of works, lest anyone should boast. For we are His workmanship, created in Christ Jesus for good works, which God prepared beforehand that we should walk in them".

Roman 10: 9-10 states that, "that if you confess with your mouth the Lord Jesus and believe in your heart that God has raised Him from the dead, you will be saved. For with the heart one believes unto righteousness, and with the mouth confession is made unto salvation"

You should ask Jesus Christ to come into your life now; to cleanse your sins away with His blood, which He shed on the Cross of Calvary; to fill you with His Holy Spirit, which He promised you and to transform your life. When Jesus Christ comes into your life, your life will never be the same as He will bring illumination and give you a fresh revelation about your life that will change your playing field. It is Jesus Christ's wish that you begin to walk in the purpose for which you were created. The Holy Spirit will guide and help you to fulfil your calling in Jesus' Name.

If you don't know what to say, you may say the following prayer now-

> *"I acknowledge that Jesus Christ came to this earth for mankind; that He died on the Cross of Calvary for me, a sinner; that He resurrected on the third day and there is power in His resurrection. I believe that Jesus Christ has redeemed me from the penalty of sin and death. I confess all my sins to Jesus and I ask Him to forgive me now, to transform me and to start a new work in my life. I ask you Jesus Christ to come into my life so that I can start to live my life for you. I thank you Lord Jesus for forgiving me all my sins and giving me eternal life. Amen.*

Once you have given your life to Christ, you must begin to read the Bible daily and pray for the Holy Spirit's guidance and direction. You should ask Him to give you spiritual understanding and enlightenment. You may wish to start reading from the Gospel of John, which explains God's love for mankind and Jesus' willingness to sacrifice Himself so that Man (including you) can be reconciled to God. You should also consider finding a local church that is Bible based if you don't already attend one. You should introduce yourself to the Pastor who will nurture you spiritually and build you up in the Lord, the same applies to those who once attended church but backslid for one reason or another, return to the Lord and He will return to you.

JESUS COMPLETED HIS ASSIGNMENT

During Jesus' crucifixion the soldiers mocked Him and called Him the King of the Jews but they did not really know the significance of what they were saying. Jesus did not relent on His purpose even unto death. His last words on the cross were *"It is finished"*. You must finish and accomplish your purpose in life before you depart to eternity. When Jesus Christ died on the cross He became the High Priest over all creation.

When Jesus Christ said it is finished, He was saying that He had accomplished, fulfilled, finalised **ALL** that God had assigned Him to do. He died to ransom man back to God and He performed His task by rising to vanquish death and live forevermore. As He rose to conquer death, this same conqueror's spirit now resides within you. Are you living a conqueror's life?

The Supremacy of Christ: - *Colossians 1: 15 -20 gives us an insight into the Supremacy of Jesus Christ, we know that by conquering death and rising to live for evermore Jesus confirmed His Supremacy over all things.* Can you also say that you have finished the race of life? Do you really understand what it means to finish your race in life? **The words "Finished" and "All" as taken from The Free Dictoniary.Com means:**

FINISHED

- To arrive at or attain the end of.
- To bring to an end; terminate
- To bring to a desired or required state
- To destroy; kill:

ALL

pron.

- The entire or total number, amount, or quantity; totality
- Everyone; everything: *justice for all.*

adv.

- Wholly; completely

Since Jesus Christ has destroyed everything that stands in your way to victory you have no reason to fail. He wants you to stand before God at the end of your tenure on earth and truly say that you totally attained and entirely completed your God given assignment.

SIMON PETER

Jesus Christ called Simon Peter whilst he was catching fish, Peter left what he was doing to follow Jesus and become fishers of men. He was one of the twelve chosen to be a special disciple and he was given the authority and power to heal the sick and to drive out demons. Peter made good use of the anointing that was bestowed upon his life.

> *"And as He walked by the Sea of Galilee, He saw Simon and Andrew his brother casting a net into the sea; for they were fishermen. Then Jesus said to them, 'Follow Me, and I will make you become fishers of men.' They immediately left their nets and followed Him" Mark 1:16-17.*

When Jesus appeared to the disciples on the boat, they saw that He was walking on the water. Peter asked Jesus to command him to come to Him on the water. Jesus did so, and Peter began to walk on the water towards Jesus until he doubted at which point he began to sink.

Here you have a glimpse of Peter's purpose; he was different from the other disciples. Although he appeared outwardly timid and lacking in confidence, he had zeal. Jesus Christ told Peter that he would deny Him three times but Peter refused to believe it, as he thought he was unshakable. Peter cried when he denied Jesus Christ before His accusers for he was truly repentant. Regret, sin and condemnation have a way of preventing you from maximizing your potential as they take hold of you but true repentance restores you.

Peter repented of his lack of inner strength and courage. His humility led to the restoration of his broken relationship with Jesus Christ. When Peter heard that Jesus had resurrected, he ran to the tomb to look for Him. When Jesus saw Peter's sincerity, He re-affirmed him to cancel the guilt of betrayal that Peter was carrying within him. Jesus Christ showed a good example by forgiving Peter, who was not deserving of it (*Matthew 26; John 21*).

You will sometimes look back and regret the actions you have taken – when you failed to strengthen, encourage or support those around you who were in need. You may feel regret and shame at your weaknesses but you must not allow these to prevent you from seeking restoration of the relationship.

Jesus Christ rewarded Peter for his steadfastness by putting him in charge of the disciples. He was not always a natural leader but the anointing for leadership came upon him to direct the affairs of the brethren; after Jesus' ascension, Peter rose up to his calling.

On the day of Pentecost when the Holy Spirit descended upon those who were worshipping God, some people made mockery of the believers who were speaking in tongues; Peter stood up with authority and confronted 'the God mockers'. Peter's boldness was apparent to others around him. He won three thousand people to Christ on that day and they were added to the Body of Christ.

Peter began walking in the full manifestation of his calling as an apostle, leader and healer. This power, which was once latent, became active. Peter who was once docile became the forerunner in spreading the Good News of Salvation. As Peter began to preach with boldness, he was thrown into jail, despite this, the church grew to five thousand people. On another occasion Peter stood up to answer his accusers who could see a new eloquence and attitude in him. You must realise that when Jesus calls us He equips us for the task ahead.

'Then Peter, [because he was] filled with [and controlled by] the Holy Spirit, said to them, Rulers of the people and

members of the council (the Sanhedrin), If we are being put on trial [here] today and examined concerning a good deed done to benefit a feeble (helpless) cripple, by what means this man has been restored to health, Let it be known and understood by all of you, and by the whole house of Israel, that in the name and through the power and authority of Jesus Christ of Nazareth, Whom you crucified, [but] Whom God raised from the dead, in Him and by means of Him this man is standing here before you well and sound in body. This [Jesus] is the Stone which was despised and rejected by you, the builders, but which has become the Head of the corner [the Cornerstone]. And there is salvation in and through no one else, for there is no other name under heaven given among men by and in which we must be saved. Now when they saw the boldness and unfettered eloquence of Peter and John and perceived that they were unlearned and untrained in the schools [common men with no educational advantages], they marvelled; and they recognized that they had been with Jesus" (Acts 4: 8-13-Amp).

God by His divine power has bestowed on each of us the skills that are necessary for us to accomplish our assignment. He has endowed us with gifts and talents that would enable us live a fruitful and productive life, it is our duty to discover these gifts so that we can accomplish our purpose (2 Peter 1:3-4).

PAUL (SAUL)

Paul was an enthusiast but his enthusiasm was focused in the wrong direction. When Stephen was killed, Paul gloried in his death and his persecution of the Christian believers was fuelled. He treated the Christians with contempt, arresting and imprisoning them for their belief in Christ.

On his way to Damascus, the Lord stopped Paul in his tracks to get his attention; he was shown the error of his ways and reprimanded by God for persecuting Him. The encounter Paul had with God completely changed his life; he began to utilize his zeal in a positive way. Barnabas went to Antioch and brought Paul back with him because he recognized the potential in Paul's life. Paul was ordained to do what God had called him to do.

At Lystra, Paul saw a man who had been crippled from birth and had never walked. Paul gazed intently at the man and shouted at him to stand up on his feet, the man was filled with faith, and stood up and walked. Paul and Barnabas were mistaken for gods but they refused to accept the glory accorded to them, which infuriated the people. Paul realized that the authority to heal the sick came from God who had empowered and equipped him; he therefore refused to elevate himself (*Acts 14: 8-18*). Paul touched handkerchiefs, towels and aprons, which were then placed on the sick and diseased who later received their healing; he also raised Eutychus from the dead when he fell out of a window to his death.

Paul realized that maturity was required in dealing with the people both outside and within the church. He was discerning enough to resolve the dispute that arose between Barnabas and himself over John Mark (*Acts 15:36-41*). He knew that the growth of the church was dependent on his ability to forgive past errors of judgment and see the potential in others around him. He therefore requested for John Mark to be brought to him later on in his ministry.

Although Paul and Barnabas constantly faced opposition, it did not hamper the movement of God's work in the life of the Gentiles they ministered to. Paul continued to reason and debate with the philosophers, using his skills as a lawyer and advocate to argue his position about the resurrection of Jesus Christ, he converted Dionysius, a judge in Areaopagus amongst other notable persons (Acts 17: 34). His ability as an orator and a public speaker was put to use in the Kingdom of God to promote the gospel of Jesus Christ.

He was focused on his assignment and did not allow others to distract him from achieving his goals. He knew that God called him to preach to the Gentiles and therefore he set his mind on that. He knew that Jesus Christ had stopped him in his tracks to become a distinguished minister of the gospel. He recognized, identified and acknowledged that God had called him out of his own comfort zone to be a channel of blessing to the body of believers (*Acts 26*).

When faced with adversity during his stormy journey on the ship, Paul knew that his destiny would not be aborted; he had God's assurance that there would be no loss of life despite what he saw. Paul knew that the God who had called him would not forsake him before the fulfilment of his purpose. The destiny Paul was carrying within him was so great that even the viper, which fastened itself around Paul's hand could not stop him. Paul shrugged off the viper and continued his mission by healing the father of Publius (*Acts 27; 28*)

In your journey through life, you are destined to meet people whose lives you will touch and transform; you should not allow adversity, trials or tribulations stop you from being a blessing. You must look at challenges as temporary hiccups that would soon clear away. You must shrug off everything that is preventing you from achieving the vision and goals that God has called you to achieve. Even when Paul was marooned on the Island, he did not allow the obstacles he faced stop him.

If you truly believe that God has called you to achieve your life's goal then do not allow distractions to hamper you. You can manoeuvre yourself around the obstacles, pick yourself up and stop the pity-party, dust the sand off your feet and begin the mile walk to your destination, you may tarry but do not give up.

Paul did not obtain Peter's or any of the other Apostles' consent when he began his ministry as he knew they would not have approved of him or even selected him because of his past reputation. It was only after he had established himself for three years that he sought an audience with Peter. His godly reputation preceded him everywhere he went, causing people to glorify God. When God calls you, He even makes those opposed to you to bring out their hands of fellowship to you publicly for your elevation (*Galatians 2:9*).

> *Once you know that it is God who has called, elected and chosen you, you will do what He has asked you to do without consulting others to seek their approval.*

"For I am already about to be sacrificed [my life is about to be poured out as a drink offering]; the time of my [spirit's] release [from the body] is at hand and I will soon go free. I have fought the good (worthy, honourable, and noble) fight, I have finished the race, I have kept (firmly held) the faith. [As to what remains] henceforth there is laid up for me the [victor's] crown of righteousness [for being right with God and doing right], which the Lord, the righteous Judge, will award to me and recompense me on that [great] day—and not to me only, but also to all those who have loved and yearned for and welcomed His appearing (His return)."2 Timothy 4: 6-8 (Amp)

Paul received a lot of opposition and had false accusations levied against him from his fellow Jews because he preached a message of hope and redemption through Jesus Christ. He was arrested and imprisoned because of his faith in Jesus Christ and because he had boldly maintained that Jesus Christ had died and was resurrected.

The Jews who were pursuing Paul did not send letters ahead of his arrival at Rome because God had frustrated their movement and actions. Paul was therefore free to continue his ministry; to keep his momentum in achieving his vision; in accomplishing his goals and in winning the prized trophy. He was able to boldly say at the end of his life that he had run the race of life and he had finished his course well!

Like Paul, those who choose to hinder you in your journey of life will tire themselves out and withdraw themselves from you, as God will frustrate them and their designs. You will surely complete the race of life. You dreams will not go unfulfilled; you will keep your faith to the end and proudly say that you have poured out everything within you as a living sacrifice.

TIMOTHY

Timothy, a protégé of Paul was a committed and dedicated follower of God. He began his ministry as an understudy of Paul who mentored and trusted him with the spiritual lives of the believers. He was sent by Paul on numerous occasions to strengthen the churches. He accompanied Paul on evangelism and ministrations. Paul saw him as a brother and son in the ministry, he encouraged Timothy to live according to the prophecy on his life.

> *"This charge I commit to you, son Timothy, according to the prophecies previously made concerning you, that by them you may wage the good warfare, having faith and a good conscience, which some having rejected, concerning the faith have suffered shipwreck" 1 Timothy 1:18.*

> *"For this reason I have sent Timothy to you, who is my beloved and faithful son in the Lord, who will remind you of my ways in Christ, as I teach everywhere in every church." 1 Corinthians 4:17.*

Timothy's attributes were notable to the churches that he came in contact with. He was considered to be a loyal and faithful believer who genuinely had the interest and growth of the church to heart. Timothy served Paul diligently and did not have an ulterior agenda of overthrowing the spiritual authority of Paul.

When Paul was hindered from going to Thessalonica, he sent Timothy ahead to prepare the way for him in spreading the gospel to the gentiles and to establish and encourage the church. Paul knew God had called Timothy to be his right hand man.

Timothy succeeded in his ministry because he listened to Paul's counsel to become all that God had created him to be. He was strong, courageous and bold in his ability and convictions; he became a distinguished minister of God.

PRISCILLA AND AQUILA

Priscilla and Aquila were a Jewish Christian couple who strengthened the church by being enablers in the body of Christ. They were associates of Apostle Paul who they accommodated when he was in Corinth. They took Appollos under their wing, built him up and instructed him in the way of the Lord, Appollos later became a powerful preacher of his time.

They chose to walk in the gifting God had placed on their lives. They used their spiritual gifts of encouragement to mentor others in the church. The church today needs encouragers who will help mould new converts to grow in the Lord (Acts 18).

TITUS

Titus was a gentile convert who accompanied Paul on his missionary journeys. He grew in the Lord under the guidance and influence of Paul. Paul referred to him as a true child who had a common purpose with him to see lives transformed and souls won for Christ. He preached sound doctrine that was unquestionable to all who heard him speak.

He started his life as an outsider, unbeliever and an uncircumcised gentile, but was found worthy to be appointed a minister to preach the gospel (*Book of Titus*).

JOHN

John wrote the Epistle of John, John 1, 2, 3 and the Book of Revelation. He was a fisherman when Jesus called him into ministry to be part of the twelve apostles. He was actively involved with Jesus' ministry from the beginning and therefore his report was from first hand knowledge of what he saw and heard.

> *"That which was from the beginning, which we have heard, which we have seen with our eyes, which we have looked upon, and our hands have handled, concerning the Word of life—the life was manifested, and we have seen, and bear witness, and declare to you that eternal life which was with the Father and was manifested to us—that which we have seen and heard we declare to you, that you also may have fellowship with us; and truly our fellowship is with the Father and with His Son Jesus Christ. And these things we write to you that your joy may be full" 1 John 1: 1-4*

John's account of Jesus Christ's life shows his unique relationship with Him. Because he received unconditional love from Jesus Christ, he was able to portray in his writings Jesus Christ's love for all mankind. He was sure of his salvation and in the miracles he saw Jesus perform. John was so close to Jesus that he rested on His bosom; he was with Jesus at His transfiguration alongside Peter and James.

John always started his Books by referring to the Word of Life. His vision of the end time came from the personal revelation he had when he was taken up into the Sprit where he was shown what would happen before the second coming of Jesus Christ.

He saw the same revelation that Daniel saw. God assured John that for those who overcame they would eat of the fruit of the tree of life in the Garden of God. John saw in his vision Jesus Christ breaking the seal which no one else was worthy to break, he was privileged to sit at the foot of the altar of the souls of those who had been scarified for God's sake. He also saw the victorious believers who were robed in white and were serving before God's Throne (*Book of Revelation*). The visions he saw are evidence that he was closely connected with God.

All the men and women mentioned in this Chapter were successful in their respective callings because they used their gifting and talents to build God's kingdom. You too must put your talents and skills to effective use in God's kingdom if you want to impact your generation.

CHAPTER 4

Living a Life of Purpose

(Receive God's Revelation to Live a Life Worthy of Your Calling)

Living a life of purpose will show that you know and understand the reason for your existence. Living a life of purpose means that despite the odds you are fulfilling God's plan for your life. You must commit your ways to the Lord and He will direct your path. God expects you to live fully so that when you depart this world you will leave your mark behind.

Here are a few quotes to remind us of what "Purpose" is:

"I learned the most important lesson of my life: that the extraordinary is not the birthright of a chosen and privileged few, but of all people, even the humblest. That is my one certainty: we are all the manifestation of the divinity of God."
Paulo Coelho

"I am here for a purpose and that purpose is to grow into a mountain, not to shrink to a grain of sand. Henceforth will I apply ALL my efforts to become the highest mountain of all and I will strain my potential until it cries for mercy."
Og Mandino

"The great and glorious masterpiece of man is to know how to live to purpose." – Michel de Montaigne

To live an exceptional, outstanding and extraordinary life, you must live purposefully. You must leave an impact on your generation too difficult to erase. When you do so, those after you will sing of your praises. The Scriptures gives us an array of notable men and women who lived exceptionally. Some of these are:-

JOSEPH

Joseph was the twelfth child and eleventh son of Jacob; he was Rachel's first child and the only full blood brother of Benjamin. At a young age Joseph received the revelation of who God had called him to be. He dreamt that his parents and brothers bowed down to him to pay him homage. When he told his brothers his dream they hated him for it because they understood its meaning — that he would someday rule over them. They felt that they should be ruling over their younger brother rather than them serving him.

"Now Joseph had a dream and he told it to his brothers, and they hated him still more. And he said to them, Listen now and hear, I pray you, this dream that I have dreamed: We [brothers] were binding sheaves in the field, and behold, my sheaf arose and stood upright, and behold, your sheaves stood round about my sheaf and bowed down! His brothers said to him, 'Shall you indeed reign over us? Or are you going to have us as your subjects and dominate us?' And they hated him all the more for his dreams and for what he said. But Joseph dreamed yet another dream and told it to his brothers [also]. He said, See here, I have dreamed again, and behold, [this time not only] eleven stars [but also] the sun and the moon bowed down and did reverence to me! And he told it to his father [as well as] his brethren. But his father rebuked him and said to him, 'What is the meaning of this dream that you have dreamed? Shall I and your mother and your brothers actually come to bow down ourselves to the earth and do homage to you?" (Genesis 37: 5-10-Amp).

After Joseph told his brothers his dreams they changed their attitude towards him. They also planned to kill him but Reuben intervened and persuaded his siblings not to kill Joseph as his blood would be upon their heads forever. God will always frustrate the plans of your enemies, He will cause a mouthpiece to rise up in their midst to fight your cause. Their hatred will not stop God performing the promises He has made to you. God knows what He is doing in your life; He will never abandon you to fate or disappoint the hope that you have of Him in coming through for you.

> "And Reuben said to them, Shed no blood, but cast him into this pit or well that is out here in the wilderness and lay no hand on him. He was trying to get Joseph out of their hands in order to rescue him and deliver him again to his father. When Joseph had come to his brothers, they stripped him of his [distinctive] long garment, which he was wearing. Then they took him and cast him into the [well-like] pit which was empty; there was no water in it" (Genesis 37:22- 24-Amp).

The stripping of Joseph's garment did not mean the stripping away of God's purpose for his life. No one can strip away God's purpose for your life. Sometimes the devil orchestrates bad things to happen to you by sabotaging your goals or by bringing people to discourage your vision; God would always give you the last laugh.

Joseph was seventeen years old when he was sold into slavery, he could have chosen to remain dejected but he chose not to. He did not resign himself to fate but aligned himself with the will of God by preparing and equipping himself with the necessary tools and skills that would be required for his future. His calling was too great for anyone to silence or cover up. Although Joseph's dream remained with him throughout his period in slavery, he excelled in Potiphar's house and was promoted as supervisor in his household.

Joseph excelled in his gifting which opened doors for him. God blessed the works of his hands and he succeeded in everything he did. Joseph also found favour in Potiphar's sight, not only did Joseph become distinguished; Potiphars' household became blessed by reason of the covenant relationship Joseph had with God. Even when he was thrown into prison, he excelled.

> *You are certainly greater than where you are right now...*

No matter what people call you or who they say that you are, you must negate their expectations of you whilst they are looking on. We want you to know that what God has placed inside of you is far greater than you can ever imagine and that no one can kill your dream unless you permit them to do so.

After Pharaoh's dream, the butler remembered Joseph and told Pharaoh about him. Joseph was able to interpret Pharaohs' dreams and was promoted on the same day. Within twenty-four hours, Joseph's testimony changed from being a slave to a Governor over the land of Egypt including the household of Portiphar who had previously put him in prison. Joseph spent thirteen years in Egypt as a slave and became Governor at the age of thirty.

God never forgot His covenant of prosperity with Joseph; He was merely waiting for Joseph to be mature enough to handle the coming blessings. God knew that for Joseph to fully achieve all that He had purposed for him, he would need to develop the skills and decorum required for the work he was called to do. He used Joseph's brothers as a training ground to cut off the excess baggage he was carrying. God also wanted Joseph to have respect and reverence for his elders so that he could understand that it was by God's grace he had been promoted and not by the works of his own hands. God took Joseph through the wilderness of life in order to build his character for such a time when he would take up the reigns of power.

Your time of remembrance and promotion will come from the Lord in its due season. When you believe that your promotion is in the hands of men you are subject to their whims and caprices. We often look to the wrong people for our blessings and that is where we go wrong as these people often disappoint and hurt us. David said in Psalms 121:1-3 that he would look up to the hills because his help comes from the Lord, Jehovah the Mighty One, who made the heavens and the earth. He realised that God would not let his foot slip, or be moved during times of hardship.

Joseph's brothers who had thought he would never amount to anything good saw the manifestation and fulfilment of his dream come to pass. When Joseph's brothers threw him in a pit they thought it would bring to an end God's purpose for his life but they forgot that God orders the footsteps of the righteous and that God had pre-determined Joseph's future before he was formed in his mother's womb. God's Word cannot be destroyed or exterminated by the actions of men (*Psalms 23: 5-6*).

Others may think you do not qualify for the promotion or the blessing but it is not for them to decide whether you qualify or not. God will certainly come through for you in a special way. You have a part to play in society. To all those who feel that time has passed them by, Joseph's turnaround is proof that it's never too late to live the dream and re-define yourself (*Genesis 39: 1-6*).

You may have been abused by your family members or relatives either physically, psychologically, emotionally or sexually and you have often wondered whether you would recover from the scars of the past; just as Joseph rose above the expectations of his brothers to become an overcomer so would you also rise to overcome and recover to fulfil God's purpose for your life. Some of you may have been told to get on with your lives as if nothing had happened and you have become down-trodden, God's healing balm will soothe your pain so that you can start living as He wants you to.

"Forgiving does not erase the bitter past. A healed memory is not a deleted memory. Instead, forgiving what we cannot forget creates a new way to remember. We change the memory of our past into a hope for our future."-Lewis B. Smedes

God will bring you out of every stronghold of the past to become a man or woman of substance. Slowly, surely and steadily the time will come when your vision will be fulfilled. You don't need to prove anything to anybody for God's appointed time will surely come.

TAMAR

Tamar married Er who was later killed by God because of his wicked ways. After Er's death, Judah told his second son Onan to marry Tamar so that she could bear an offspring for Er. However, Onan did not want to father a child through her for his brother so he prevented conception when he had sex with her, and the Lord saw his deception and killed him.

Judah became scared that his youngest son Shelah would suffer the same fate, he therefore told Tamar to remain a widow at her father's house until Shelah grew up and was old enough to marry her. Judah knew that by that time Tamar would be too old to marry him.

After a period of time, Judah's wife died and he sought the comfort of a loose woman, unbeknown to him the woman was his daughter-in-law (Tamar). When Tamar saw Judah she hatched a plan to become pregnant with his child so she slept with him and kept his signet ring, bracelet and staff as evidence of their one night stand together. Three months later when Judah was told that Tamar was pregnant, he planned to humiliate and disgrace her by burning her to death. She embarrassed him instead by producing his signet ring, bracelet and staff as her evidence that he was the father of her child. Judah had to acknowledge that Tamar was more honourable than he was because he had not kept his promise of giving Shelah to her as was customary in their culture.

Tamar knew her own worth and her rights as a bereaved daughter-in-law in Judah's household; she knew Judah had failed in his responsibility to provide a covering over her as the head of his clan. By her courageous act, she found herself included in the gospel of Mathew as one of the five women in the genealogy of Jesus Christ.

Tamar like many today had been sexually abused by the men in her family. She boldly took her destiny into her own hands by speeding up the process of claiming her possessions. She pre-empted her accusers and rode on their backs to her destiny (Genesis 38).

You must discover your true self, the person God has created you to be and become that person. Know who you are in God and don't allow others to define, nullify or limit you. Your decision to step out of the box will change the course of your destiny. **You were created by God to live a life of purpose and meaning**, so don't settle for second best.

MOSES

The Pharaoh ruling at the time Moses was born decreed that the midwives were to kill the Hebrew male children at birth. However the midwives disobeyed his decree and allowed the male children to live thereby safeguarding the life of Moses. Moses' mother hid him for three months before laying him in a basket amongst the bushes at the brink of the river where he was found by Pharaoh's daughter who adopted him as her own and called him Moses meaning to "draw out".

When Moses grew up he killed an Egyptian man whom he saw beating a fellow Hebrew brother. Because of this, he had to flee Egypt to a place where he remained for forty years until it was God's time to act. Moses had been rescued by Pharaoh's daughter, so he too prematurely wanted to be a rescuer of his people. As human beings, we sometimes feel that God is too slow to act so we take matters into our own hands. It is best to wait for God to direct us and to go in His direction rather than against it. After forty years of being in the wilderness, God appeared to Moses in a flame of fire out of the midst of the bush and spoke with him about the covenant relationship He had with his predecessors and that He was there to fulfil His Word.

"And when the Lord saw that he turned aside to see, God called to him out of the midst of the bush and said, Moses, Moses! And he said, 'Here am I.' God said, Do not come near; put your shoes off your feet, for the place on which you stand is holy ground. Also He said, I am the God of your father, the God of Abraham, the God of Isaac, and the God of Jacob… Come now therefore, and I will send you to Pharaoh, that you may bring forth My people, the Israelites, out of Egypt. And Moses said to God, Who am I, that I should go to Pharaoh and bring the Israelites out of Egypt? God said, I will surely be with you; and this shall be the sign to you that I have sent you: … Moses said to God, Behold, when I come to the Israelites and say to them, The God of your fathers has sent me to you, and they say to me, What is His name? What shall I say to them? And God said to Moses, I AM WHO I AM and WHAT I AM, and I WILL BE WHAT I WILL BE; and He said, You shall say this to the Israelites: I AM has sent me to you! God said also to Moses, This shall you say to the Israelites: The Lord, the God of your fathers, of Abraham, of Isaac, and of Jacob, has sent me to you! This is My name forever, and by this name I am to be remembered to all generations" (Exodus 3: 4-15-Amp).

God spoke to Moses about the specific assignment He wanted him to fulfil but by this time Moses had given up his vision of being an activist so he replied, "Who am I that I should be asked to undertake such a task" Moses had developed an identity crisis because he had failed to achieve success in his own strength. He felt that he no longer had the zeal to pursue his dreams because he had gone off course for too long and it was impossible for him to get back on the right track. He knew that he was born a Hebrew but he had lived the life of an Egyptian prince. He had wanted to help his Hebrew people but they had rejected him, worse still the Egyptians did not want him around them either; he felt he was a misfit not having being accepted by either side.

"Who Am I" is a question that every individual ponders on at some point in his or her life. You may be in a relationship where you are being abused and you ask yourself *"Who Am I"*. You may have lived your life for your spouse or children and they have now moved on and left you behind. You may feel that you have sacrificed your time or yourself for someone who did not value you and now you wonder whether this is what life is all about and you ask yourself *"Who Am I"*.

WHO I AM IN GOD

God in His infinite wisdom pre-empted that you might at some stage ask yourself this question so He has provided you with answers in anticipation of them. God's response to you is:

- You are a child of God- John 1:12

- You are a branch of Jesus Christ, the true vine, and a channel of His life- John 15:5

- You have been justified and redeemed by God -Romans 3: 24

- You are no longer condemned by God – Romans 8:1

- You are a joint heir with Jesus Christ- Romans 8: 17

- You are God's temple and His Spirit dwells permanently in you- I Corinthians 3:16

- You are God's temple, you were bought with a price and you belong to God- I Corinthians 6:19- 20

- You are part of Jesus Christ's body- 1 Corinthians 12:27

- You are a new creature in Jesus Christ – 2 Corinthians 5: 17

- You have been chosen, selected and adopted by God as His child- Ephesians 1:3-8

- You are blessed with every spiritual blessing in the Heavenly Realm- Ephesians 1:3

- You were predestined by God through Jesus Christ to obtain a Godly inheritance – Ephesians 1:11

- You are seated with Jesus Christ in the Heavenly Realm- Ephesians 2:6

- You are strong in the Lord – Ephesians 6:10

- You are a citizen of heaven- Philippians 3: 20

- You are hidden in Christ in God- Colossians 3:1-4

- You are victorious – Revelation: 21: 7

You can see that God has chosen, selected and adopted you as His very own. You are certainly not a mistake or accident of pro-creation as some may want you to believe or think.

Moses had wondered how God would want to send a person like him to Pharaoh, perhaps he felt God did not know or realise who Pharaoh was! When you ask God how He can use someone like you or how He can send you to minister, prophesy or evangelise to another person you are undermining and underestimating Him. If God had thought you were incapable of being sent He would not have assigned the job to you in the first place. You must stop believing that you are not worthy or that you do not qualify because of your past mistakes, failures or weaknesses. Moses dealt with the same struggles that you are facing today but he still qualified for the job.

Moses was also posing the following questions to God, a) are you asking me to go to my people- the Hebrew people who have rejected me as one of their number and b) are you asking me to return to the Egyptians — who consider me a traitor and filth in their eyes? Moses was afraid to go to Egypt, a land that was prosperous and intimidating; the great land which held his blessings. God knew what plans He had for Moses, He was sending Moses back to Egypt to deal with his past, which he was running away from. When Moses left Egypt the first time, he had left empty handed, in shame and with bad memories, God wanted Moses to leave there a second time with dignity and honour so that he could put his past behind him and walk into a brighter future (Proverbs 4:18).

To assure Moses, God told him that He would be with him and identified Himself to Moses as, "*I AM WHO I AM and WHAT I AM, and I WILL BE WHAT I WILL BE*"

God's Name is "I AM WHO I AM and WHAT I AM, and I WILL BE WHAT I WILL BE"

God widened Moses' mind that **He Is** the infinite, unrivalled and unequalled God, the God who was at Moses' beginning and knows his ending. The God who was, who is today and whose supreme reign will remain forever. God told Moses that he could only find his real identity in Him and no other. He was revealing the Worth, Essence and Power behind His Name, which Moses could not seem to comprehend.

When God identified Himself to Moses He was telling Moses that He is faithful, reliable, dependable, merciful, gracious, slow to anger and abounding in love. God was telling Moses that He would become anything He chose to be to ensure that Moses fulfilled his God given assignment in life. God was also telling Moses that He is the Eternal God, The Saviour, The Holy and Righteous One; His Lord and God, The God of All Grace; His Lord and King, His Creator, The God of Power and Might and The Most High God. We must not limit God in our thinking because of our past experiences but we should expand our mind to accommodate the fullness of God. What more do you want from the God that you serve?

God does not suffer from identity crises like we often do; there is no variation in Him. You too must understand that your identity comes from God and not from man, as men sometimes portray a bad reflection of God. If the people you look up to are flawed, then you will automatically assume that God too is flawed. God is waiting for you to come to the understanding that He is all that you will ever need to have a fulfilled life. Once you receive this revelation you will stop running after people who don't value you at all. No matter where you have been or what you might have done God is waiting for you to know Him personally as your ALL in ALL.

When you open your heart to receive God and all He has in store for you, you will operate in your anointing. You will walk in another dimension and operate on a different playing field from your contemporaries, as real changes will occur in your life. **There are many men and women in the Bible whose lives would not have amounted to anything but for the choices and decisions they made and the faith actions they took to enter into the purpose they were born for.**

When God sends us on assignment we should see what God is seeing. Pharaoh might have appeared formidable and untouchable but to God he was conquerable. God told Moses He had never changed and that He is a never changing God. The fact that Moses did not recognise or acknowledge God as All Powerful does not mean that He is not all-powerful.

The fact that you have not recognised or acknowledged your potential, gifting or calling does not mean that you do not have them. God is waiting for you to receive the revelation of who He has created you to be. You have been equipped with all that you will ever need in your life's journey. People are sometimes surprised at their ability; they fail to realise that the ability to be creative and to be successful had been placed inside of them by God but they had failed to identify their potential.

> *Identify and utilise the skills, gifts and talents lying dormant within you.*

Moses feared that if he told the Israelites that God had sent him, they would laugh at him. God wants you to activate the faith within you. Moses had a rod, what do you have in your hands that can be used to build up your family, community and local church. God has implanted and impregnated you with varying abilities, gifting, talents and strengths. It is your duty to rise up and utilise them.

You may ask how can you start doing the things God has called you to do? We suggest you start by doing things little by little and taking a day at a time! If you are the shy or introvert type, you can become a steward in your local church and join a department like ushering, welcome team or meeters and greeters where you would be the first point of call. You would soon discover that you are developing your people skills on how to relate to others.

Many think they can't achieve or fulfil what they have yearned to attain because they don't have the necessary skills at the moment, Moses felt that way too! Once God has placed a yearning within you, He will equip you. God knows the calling that best fits your character and He will direct your path from an early age so that as you mature in Him you will blend automatically into your purpose. The transition may be gradual but it will manifest itself in due season.

Moses succeeded in delivering the Israelites out of the hands of Pharaoh because he listened to God. Moses led the Israelites through the wilderness towards the Promised Land, depending on God for their sustenance. They eventually sinned prolonging their journey by forty years. Although Moses did not physically enter the Promised Land because of his disobedience, God allowed him to see it. This showed the extent of the relationship God had with Moses that despite his error of judgement, God was still merciful and gracious to him, allowing Moses to rest in peace knowing that he had seen Israel's inheritance.

RAHAB

Rahab was a woman whose destiny was wrongly determined because of her profession (prostitution). She found herself in the lineage of King David and Jesus Christ by her act of courage in hiding the two spies sent from Shittim by Joshua. She hid these men away in her roof from the men who were sent by the King of Jericho to arrest them because of her faith in the God of Israel who was able to preserve her family and herself when the destruction of Jericho takes place. She pleaded with the two spies to show kindness to her and they gave her a sign of their promise. The spies took an oath to protect her provided she kept their secret and did not give them up.

> "Now therefore, I beg you, swear to me by the LORD, since I
> have shown you kindness, that you also will show kindness
> to my father's house, and give me a true token, and spare my
> father, my mother, my brothers, my sisters, and all that they
> have, and deliver our lives from death." So the men answered
> her, "Our lives for yours, if none of you tell this business of
> ours. And it shall be, when the LORD has given us the land,
> that we will deal kindly and truly with you." Joshua 2:12-14.

Rahab let the spies down on a rope through her window and told them to hide for three days in the mountains. The spies gave her a scarlet cord to tie on her window, which will be a sign for Joshua and the Israelites. As a harlot, she would have been the last person to be reckoned with, however God chose her to bring deliverance to His people. You must not judge, condemn or conclude too early that a person is beyond redemption or transformation.

She was a woman of no repute, an outcast having engaged in the oldest profession of her time, which she conducted on the walls of Jericho by servicing every traveller that came through the gates of Jericho but God overlooked her past because He saw the humility of her heart and her desire to please Him. Rahab must have gone on to share her testimony with fellow prostitutes and told them that they too can be transformed, changed and cleaned up.

Rahab must have had great dreams as a youngster but her dreams were temporarily shattered by the circumstances of life in which she had found herself. However she did not give up her hope of a better future. She was compensated for her past accordingly. She called upon God to rescue both herself and her family and God came through for her.

There are many who may have lived the lifestyle of Rahab and wonder whether they can be of any use to the kingdom of God. Just as God needed Rahab to transform and give hope to others in her situation, He also needs you to become a testimony to others. **Call upon God and He will hear you, He will turn things around for your benefit and give you a life of purpose**.

RUTH

Elimelech took his wife- Naomi, his two sons- Mahlon and Chilion and migrated to Moab from Bethlehem of Judah because of famine in the land. After his death, his sons took Moabite wives- Orpah and Ruth. Ten years afterwards, both sons died and Naomi was left with Ruth and Orpah, her daughters-in-law. Naomi decided to return to Bethlehem of Judah where the famine had now ended.

On their journey she asked her daughters-in-law to return to their families. Orpah returned home but Ruth elected to go with Naomi because she had adopted the Israelites as her own people and the God of Israel as her God.

> "And she said, "Look, your sister-in-law has gone back to her people and to her gods; return after your sister-in-law." But Ruth said: " Entreat me not to leave you, Or to turn back from following after you; For wherever you go, I will go; And wherever you lodge, I will lodge; Your people shall be my people, And your God, my God. Where you die, I will die; and there will I be buried. The LORD do so to me, and more also, If anything but death parts you and me." When she saw that she was determined to go with her, she stopped speaking to her." Ruth 1: 15-18.

Naomi had a kinsman from her husband's family named Boaz, who noticed Ruth's dedication, commitment and love towards Naomi. He told his reapers to allow Ruth to glean amongst them and not to disturb her. Ruth listened to the advice of Naomi and kept close to Boaz, which resulted in Boaz taking special notice of her, he later redeemed her from her nearest kinsman by marrying her.

In Ruth's case we see a unique relationship between herself and Naomi. Christians should aspire to achieve this level of relationship with their in-laws. Naomi was impressed with Ruth's conduct and character that she chose the wealthiest member of her family as a suitor for Ruth. Ruth would not have had the opportunity otherwise to marry such a man as Boaz. She married a settled man who gave her all that she required to live a peaceful life.

Boaz was a man of honour who was highly esteemed by the elders; we know this because he sat with the rulers at the city gate. He did not shy away from his responsibilities, he was not afraid to allow his first child to be called the offspring of Mahlon, Ruth's late husband, according to the custom in Israel.

'And all the people who were at the gate, and the elders, said, "We are witnesses. The LORD make the woman who is coming to your house like Rachel and Leah, the two who built the house of Israel; and may you prosper in Ephrathah and be famous in Bethlehem. May your house be like the house of Perez, whom Tamar bore to Judah, because of the offspring which the LORD will give you from this young woman" Ruth 4:11-12.

Not only was Ruth blessed by her mother-in-law, she was also blessed by the elders of Israel. Although God had said no Moabite shall enter his presence, He however made Ruth an exception. Ruth entered the lineage of Jesus Christ by her act of faith in the true God of Israel. Ruth's destiny changed when she elected to go with Naomi. Ruth gave birth to Obed, the father of Jesse, who was the father of David, the ancestor of Jesus Christ. Who would have thought that God had a great purpose for Ruth?

When you stick to the people God has connected you with, their success will become your success. You will find yourself being transformed gradually into the likeness and image of God. Ruth took on a new image in God and became part of His adopted children.

DAVID

David, who was God's choice for Saul's replacement, was overlooked by Samuel, the Prophet of God on the day of his ordination because he did not fit Samuel's perception of what a king should look like. He was overlooked by his father who did not remember his existence on the day of his promotion as king because he was conceived by his mother in shame. Furthermore, his brothers saw him as a nuisance because he did not look, behave or appear right. God however saw David's heart and knew that he fitted the king's seat perfectly; God wanted a man who would listen to advice or accept correction when admonished.

David's promotion started in the presence of his family and household who had thought he would not succeed. God's criteria for success are different from the standards set by the world.

> *But the LORD said to Samuel, "Do not look at his appearance or at his physical stature, because I have refused him. For the LORD does not see as man sees; for man looks at the outward appearance, but the LORD looks at the heart." ... And the LORD said, "Arise, anoint him; for this is the one!" Then Samuel took the horn of oil and anointed him in the midst of his brothers; and the Spirit of the LORD came upon David from that day forward. So Samuel arose and went to Ramah" 1 Samuel 16:7-13-NKJV.*

Being led by the flesh is different from being used by the Spirit of God. The anointing oil spoke up for David because it couldn't remain silent. David was secretly ordained as the future king and he continued to do what he had been doing before. He ministered to the wishes of Saul and did not overstep his boundaries or disregard Saul's position. He knew that God had chosen him without any physical strength on his part and so he was determined not to run ahead of God but to wait for God's appointed time to ascend the Throne.

When Goliath came out to fight Israel, David put himself forward to challenge him. He knew that God had placed him in the position to confront Goliath and he declined Saul's offer to wear his regalia to fight Goliath because he knew he was fighting in the might of God. As he ran towards Goliath he remembered how far God had brought him and how he had defeated a lion and a bear. He ran to defeat Goliath with the skills God had given him, having mastered his skills behind the scenes. He knew that God was greater, mightier and stronger that Goliath. He remembered the dreams he had whilst he tendered the sheep, he knew that the plans God had for him were greater than what people around him could envisage or imagine. When Goliath fell David saw all the obstacles in his own life fall away as well as he knew that God has set him up for his promotion (*1 Samuel 17:45-51*).

God elevated David that day in the presence of Israel's greatest enemy. You succeed in life not because you are intelligent but because you have God on your side that sets things in motion for your promotion and advancement. God brought David from tending sheep to the forefront. As a result of his victory, the Israelite women sang and praised God for using David to gain victory over their enemy causing Saul to sit up and take note of David. Saul realised that there was another contender to the Throne who had the hearts of the people; he therefore hated David from that day.

God saved David from Saul's wrath on many occasions. He never ceased to consult God before embarking on any project, his reverence of God ensured his continuous victory over his enemies.

David wept openly at the death of Saul and Jonathan; he did not promote the Amalekite who boasted that he had slain Saul but killed him for bringing an evil report. David's humility showed in the way he honoured both Saul and Jonathan after their death when he sent written praise to the men of Jabesh-Gilead for showing mercy to Saul in their burial of him. Even after he sat on the Throne of Israel, David remained true to himself, he humbled himself before God and was not ashamed to publicly dance and worship God to the dismay of his wife.

God turned Abner's loyalty from Ish-bosheth and Saul's household to David when Ish-bosheth accused Abner of sleeping with Rizpah, his father's concubine. Abner vowed to transfer the kingdom from Saul's house to David. The strongest enemy of David swore that he would give the kingship of Israel into David's hand as God had promised. (*2 Samuel 3:7-18*).

Although God did not allow David to build Him a Temple, He covenanted to permit Solomon to do so. God sent Nathan, the prophet to tell David that his kingdom will be established forever and that his descendants shall sit on his throne forever. This prophecy applied not to Solomon who reigned after him but to Jesus Christ who came to the world as a result of this promise to reign supreme (Psalm 132:11). God's covenant of blessings to David was too awesome for him to comprehend that he sat in the Temple and wept before God. He knew that when he died and went to his resting place his descendants would never cease to walk on the face of the earth. David also remembered how far he had come, he knew that God had sanctified and separated him before he was born to rule Israel. He knew that God had altered the course of his life for the better, because God had delighted in him (*2 Samuel 22*).

"When your days are fulfilled and you rest with your fathers, I will set up your seed after you, who will come from your body, and I will establish his kingdom. He shall build a house for My name, and I will establish the throne of his kingdom forever. I will be his Father, and he shall be My son. If he commits iniquity, I will chasten him with the rod of men and with the blows of the sons of men. But My mercy shall not depart from him, as I took it from Saul, whom I removed from before you. And your house and your kingdom shall be established forever before you. Your throne shall be established forever. Then King David went in and sat before the LORD; and he said: "Who am I, O Lord GOD? And what is my house, that You have brought me this far? And yet this was a small thing in Your sight, O Lord GOD; and You have also spoken of Your servant's house for a great while to come. Is this the manner of man, O Lord GOD? Now what more can David say to You? For You, Lord GOD, know Your servant. For Your word's sake, and according to Your own heart, You have done all these great things, to make Your servant know them. Therefore You are great, O Lord GOD. For there is none like You, nor is there any God besides You, according to all that we have heard with our ears." 2 Samuel 7: 12-22

David had a humble heart — when confronted by Prophet Nathan after sinning with Bathsheba and killing Uriah, her husband, he repented of his transgression. He did not seek to hide his sins like Saul did before him. Although he lived with the consequences of his actions, God forgave him. He was a man of covenant, he remembered the promises he made with Jonathan and asked his servants if there was anyone left of the household of Saul that he could bless. Mephiboseth, the cripple was brought before David and David permitted him to sit at the table and dine with him and his princes.

He died at a good old age, in prosperity, riches and honour. The City of David still remains till today as a reminder of David's service to Israel (1 Chronicles 28 and 29)

MEPHIBOSETH

Mephiboseth was the son of Jonathan and grandson of Saul. He was five years old when his nurse fled Jezreel after she heard of the death of Jonathan and Saul. He became lame in his feet after he was dropped by his house cleaner, he lived hidden away until he was brought before King David.

His life changed when David remembered his covenant with Jonathan. He was brought before David who adopted him as one of his own sons, he sat to dine at the table with the Princes and his physical condition was not obvious to anyone present. He was born into wealth and David ensured that he continued that way.

> "So David said to him, "Do not fear, for I will surely show you kindness for Jonathan your father's sake, and will restore to you all the land of Saul your grandfather; and you shall eat bread at my table continually." Then he bowed himself, and said, "What is your servant, that you should look upon such a dead dog as I?"... "As for Mephibosheth," said the king, "he shall eat at my table like one of the king's sons."

Mephibosheth had a young son whose name was Micha… So Mephibosheth dwelt in Jerusalem, for he ate continually at the king's table. And he was lame in both his feet." (2 Samuel 9: 7-13-NKJV).

King David temporarily demoted Mephiboseth and had everything taken away from him when Ziba, his servant gave a false report to David as he was fleeing the city that Mephiboseth was in support of Absalom's revolt. When David returned to the city of David, Mephiboseth came out to welcome him back, having listened to his explanation David realised that he may have judged him too harshly and partially restored his inheritance to him. It must have been because of his humility in coming to David to rejoice over his victory that David gave him a second chance to test his commitment and loyalty. When David handed over seven sons of Saul to the Gibeonites to atone for their father's sin he spared Mephiboseth because of the covenant relationship he had entered with Jonathan (*2 Samuel 21: 1-7*).

OBED-EDOM THE GILLITE

Obed-Edom was a Levitical porter who prospered because he willingly received the Ark of God into his house when King David abandoned the Ark after the death of Uzzah, who was struck by God for reaching out his hand to steady the Ark.

"David was afraid of the LORD that day; and he said, "How can the ark of the LORD come to me?" So David would not move the ark of the LORD with him into the City of David; but David took it aside into the house of Obed-Edom the Gittite. The ark of the LORD remained in the house of the Gittite three months. And the LORD blessed Obed-Edom and all his household. Now it was told King David, saying, 'The LORD has blessed the house of Obed-Edom and all that belongs to him, because of the ark of God.' So David went

and brought up the ark of God from the house of Obed-Edom to the City of David with gladness" 2 Samuel 6:9-12.

Obed-Edom had reverence for God and the things that were Holy. He became prominent because of his act of courage in allowing the Ark of God to take residence in his house for three months. God blessed him and his household to the extent that David became jealous when he heard the report of God's favour on his life. David went up to Obed-Edom's house to reclaim the Ark because he realised that without God's presence he was nothing.

To have people envious of you is one thing, but to have the King of Israel envious of your progress is another matter. King David's reaction showed that God is not a respecter of persons. He does not look at a person's status before choosing to promote him, all God requires is a heart of worship and praise. God will never forget your labour of love and sacrifice.

God blessed Obed-Edom, his children and grand children. His sons became notable gatekeepers in the house of the Lord. Obed-Edom's household grew strong in the Lord and sixty-two of them dedicated their lives to minister in the House of the Lord (*1 Chronicles 26:4-8*).

THE FOUR LEPERS AT THE CITY GATE OF SAMARIA

The four lepers at the City Gate who had been excluded from entering the city because of their leprosy were used by God to bring abundance of food to Israel. They were least expected to be courageous because of their debilitating physical condition caused by leprosy but they shocked the people of Israel by running into the enemy's camp to posses the abundant blessings that God had promised Israel. They believed that God would supply their needs from the abundance of food that was inside the camp of the Syrian army who had gathered to fight them and they were not wrong.

God upheld their faith by choosing to use the foolish things of this world to usher in the miracle prophesied by Elisha.

> *"Now there were four leprous men at the entrance of the gate; and they said to one another, "Why are we sitting here until we die? If we say, 'We will enter the city,' the famine is in the city, and we shall die there. And if we sit here, we die also. Now therefore, come, let us surrender to the army of the Syrians. If they keep us alive, we shall live; and if they kill us, we shall only die. And they rose at twilight to go to the camp of the Syrians; and when they had come to the outskirts of the Syrian camp, to their surprise no one was there. For the Lord had caused the army of the Syrians to hear the noise of chariots and the noise of horses—the noise of a great army; so they said to one another, …And when these lepers came to the outskirts of the camp, they went into one tent and ate and drank, and carried from it silver and gold and clothing, and went and hid them; then they came back and entered another tent, and carried some from there also, and went and hid it" 2 Kings 7: 3-8.*

These four men did not conform to the expectations of what their countrymen had expected from them as outcasts. They refused to fold their arms in defeat rather they took matters into their own hands to change the course of their lives. They wanted to do something so awesome that Israel would rise up and take notice of them.

God used the lepers' stumps and shackles that were on their feet to sound like the thundering noise of an approaching great army to panic the Syrian army out of their camp causing the Syrians to leave everything they had behind.

Like these lepers, you too must understand that God will use you when you are still imperfect. You must fulfil God's mandate for your life despite setbacks. God wants you to rise up with faith in your heart and take hold of all that He has promised for you.

JABEZ

Jabez from the tribe of Judah was more honourable than his brothers but his mother had given him a bad name that destined him for poverty and destruction. His name meant "sorrow" because she had given birth to him in pain. Jabez refused to settle for failure or adopt his mother's prophecy. Rather, he went to the Lord and cried to God to change his name and destiny. He said a heartfelt prayer, which should be used by every believer today. Jabez's prayer caused God to enlarge and prosper him. You must fulfil your God given purpose despite the obstacles placed in your path by others.

> *"Jabez was more honourable than his brothers. His mother had named him Jabez, saying, "I gave birth to him in pain." Jabez cried out to the God of Israel, "Oh that you would bless me and enlarge my territory! Let your hand be with me, and keep me from harm so that I will be free from pain,' and God granted his request" (1Chronicles 4: 9-10-NIV).*

Jabez came from the tribe of Judah whose lineage God had destined for greatness. He knew his heritage, that he was from a tribe of warriors who defeated their enemies, he therefore prayed for the manifestation of this blessing in his life (*1 Chronicles 5:2*). No matter how little or insignificant the beginning of a person might be, God has the power to change that person's destiny from being one of a non-entity to one of prominence. Understand that God has freed you from every limitation and everything that has hedged, curtailed or restricted your progress in life (*Psalm 4: 1*).

ESTHER

King Ahasuerus of Persia sacked Queen Vashti, his wife for humiliating him in the presence of his princes and eunuchs for refusing to come before him as his prized object. He then sought another woman to replace her and consulted his officers to seek out young maidens for training by Hegai, the king's Consul who was later to present the chosen maiden to the King.

Esther, a Jew was amongst these maidens, she found favour in Hegai's eyes, despite being in captivity. God caused Esther's light to shine before Hegai who speeded up her treatment and located her to the best harem. She obeyed Mordecai's (her uncle) counsel not to disclose her nationally at that stage. When it was Esther's turn to appear before King Ahasuerus, she requested nothing of him but only what her consul, Hegai suggested. She won the favour of the king, who loved her more than the other women who appeared before him, and he set the royal crown upon her head and made her Queen.

> "Now when the turn came for Esther ... she requested nothing but what Hegai the king's eunuch, the custodian of the women, advised. And Esther obtained favour in the sight of all who saw her... The king loved Esther more than all the other women, and she obtained grace and favour in his sight more than all the virgins; so he set the royal crown upon her head and made her queen instead of Vashti." Esther 2:15-17.

Sometime later Mordicai came to Esther with a problem concerning the Jews; in response Esther called for three days of fasting. She later approached the king on the advice of Mordecai to seek his favour to save and preserve her people. The king drew his royal sceptre to permit Esther into his presence. This was the favour of the Lord, as Esther had not followed the protocol of the palace. She requested that Haman be invited to dinner so that she can raise her concerns at the meeting. Haman was subsequently hanged for his plot to exterminate the Jews.

Esther was obedient to her uncle and remained faithful to him, her character coupled with her beauty made room for her in the palace. Although Esther's beginning was small her ending was great. She rose to prominence in a foreign land by her godly actions. She preserved her people because of her commitment, dedication and loyalty. Wherever you find yourself, it is pertinent that you seek the prosperity of the land that you are in. When your resident country is financially buoyant, you will benefit from its success.

MORDECAI

Mordecai was taken into captivity to Persia where he served the rulers of the land. Despite being in captivity he served his masters diligently. He mentored Esther and taught her how to conduct herself before Hegai, the king's consul. He sat daily at the king's gate and heard the plot made by Bigthana and Teresh (king's eunuchs), to kill the king.

Mordecai later provoked Haman to anger by not bowing down and paying him homage. Haman became obsessed with destroying Mordecai that he lost his focus, he then sought to destroy the Jews when he realised that Mordecai was one. He did not realise that God was setting him up to fail.

In the night, prior to Haman attending the banquet in the palace the Lord caused King Ahasuerus to have a dream. In the morning the King requested the Book of Memorable Deeds be brought before him where he discovered that Mordecai had not been honoured for saving his life, on that same day the King sought to promote Mordecai.

> "When Haman entered, the king asked him, "What should be done for the man the king delights to honour?" Now Haman thought to himself, "Who is there that the king would rather honour than me?" So he answered the king, "For the man the king delights to honour, have them bring a royal robe the king has worn and a horse the king has ridden, one with a royal crest placed on its head. Then let the robe and horse be entrusted to one of the king's most noble princes. Let them robe the man the king delights to honour, and lead him on the horse through the city streets, proclaiming before

him, 'This is what is done for the man the king delights to honour!' " "Go at once," the king commanded Haman. "Get the robe and the horse and do just as you have suggested for Mordecai the Jew, who sits at the king's gate. Do not neglect anything you have recommended." So Haman got the robe and the horse. He robed Mordecai, and led him on horseback through the city streets, proclaiming before him, "This is what is done for the man the king delights to honour!" (Esther 6:6-11-NIV).

Haman appeared before the king believing that the king wanted to promote him. The king asked for his suggestions on the best gift to bestow on a loyal subject. Haman proudly chose the most dignified gift. He unknowingly assisted in choosing a dignified blessing for Mordecai. Mordecai found favour in the king's sight, who gave him his signet ring as a symbol of power and authority. He was permitted in the King's name to change the laws passed to destroy the Jews. He wrote decrees that allowed the Jews to rise up to destroy their enemies.

Although Mordecai was in physical captivity he was not held captive in his mind; he knew that wherever he found himself that God had placed him there for a purpose. He rose above his station in life by being obedient to God and by showing dedication to his rulers and leaders. He held himself accountable and responsible to those above him and was rewarded accordingly for his faithfulness. His beginning was insignificant but his end was great, God took Mordecai from being a gatekeeper of the palace gates into the palace itself. God had placed him at the gate so that he can observe those who went in and came out in order to become familiar with their custom and etiquette in preparation of his promotion.

When God wants to bless you, He will cause those who oppose you to lift you up. Our God of favour would cause even our worse enemy to seek our promotion. Your day of elevation is in God's hand, so don't fret when days, weeks and months are passing you by. God's hand will reach you wherever you are to uplift you before men.

EBED-MELECH

Ebed-Melech, the Ethiopian, a Cushite was used by God to deliver Prophet Jeremiah out of the dungeon, in which he had been thrown into by King Zedekiah, (*Jeremiah 38:6-13*).

Ebed-Melech confronted the king about the way his subjects had treated Jeremiah and asked for his pardon. The king listened to him and gave him authority to release Jeremiah. He brought Jeremiah out of the pit and he took Jeremiah's worn garments off him and clothed him with decent clothing.

Ebed-Melech was not afraid to stand up and speak out against those who had imprisoned the prophet of God. He removed the clothing of shame, which Jeremiah wore and replaced them with garments of dignity. Because Ebed-Melech had put his trust, hope and faith in the Lord, the Lord sent Jeremiah to him to tell him that his enemies would not overpower him.

> *"Meanwhile the word of the LORD had come to Jeremiah while he was shut up in the court of the prison, saying, "Go and speak to Ebed-Melech the Ethiopian, saying, 'Thus says the LORD of hosts, the God of Israel: "Behold, I will bring My words upon this city for adversity and not for good, and they shall be performed in that day before you. But I will deliver you in that day," says the LORD, "and you shall not be given into the hand of the men of whom you are afraid. For I will surely deliver you, and you shall not fall by the sword; but your life shall be as a prize to you, because you have put your trust in Me,' says the LORD" (Jeremiah 39: 15-18-KJV).*

God looks at the heart of men when He seeks to promote them, because Ebed-Melech feared and honoured the prophet of God, the Lord stood up and blessed him. He became a prized instrument for all to see.

DANIEL

Daniel chose to distinguish himself from the other noble children of Israel by not defiling himself with drink or indulging himself with the food offered to them rather he chose to discipline his mind, body and spirit. Because of Daniel's commitment to living a life of purity, he found favour with Ashpenaz who allowed him and his friends to eat a diet of vegetables and water (*Daniel 1: 8-16*).

Daniel and his friends also found favour in the sight of God who gave them knowledge, skill, ability in learning and wisdom. Furthermore, Daniel had the gift of the interpretation of dreams and visions. When the time arrived for the king to converse with the youths, he found no others like Daniel and his friends; he found them ten times wiser, better and healthier than his magicians and enchanters in the land.

During the second year of his reign, king Nebuchadnezzar had a dream, which troubled him, he sought the counsel of his magicians, enchanters, soothsayers, sorcerers and diviners but they could not interpret the meaning of his dream, which he could not himself remember. The king threatened to kill his advisers if they could not tell him his dream and its interpretation. They responded by saying that no man on earth had the power to interpret a dream when he does not know it. When Daniel heard of it, he spoke to Arioch; the king's chief executioner about the matter. Daniel then went urgently to the king who gave him a set time and date to interpret his dream.

Daniel sought God's face and intervention; he knew that God had the power to bring to remembrance dreams and visions of the night season. He praised God for being faithful towards him. He knew God would show him the answers to the king's predicament.

He asked his friends to stand in prayer with him. He was wise to have like-minded people around him who sharpened his mind and spirit. Daniel acknowledged, worshipped and trusted God to carry out his purpose for him in due season.

God showed Daniel the secret of the dream and its meaning. Daniel in turn explained the dream to King Nebuchadnezzar and told him about God's plan for Babylon in the future. He told the King that God would raise other kingdoms- the Medo-Persian, Greek and Roman Empires in its place. King Nebuchadnezzar was awe stricken that Daniel knew the interpretation of the dream. He bowed to Daniel and acknowledged that Daniel served the True and Living God. He promoted Daniel as head over the whole province of Babylon and Chief Governor over all the wise men of Babylon. Daniel asked the king to promote Shadrach, Meshach and Abednego over the affairs of the province of Babylon.

> *You need prayer warriors to stand in the gap for you to petition God on your behalf.*

> *"Then King Nebuchadnezzar fell on his face, prostrate before Daniel, and commanded that they should present an offering and incense to him. The king answered Daniel, and said, "Truly your God is the God of gods, the Lord of kings, and a revealer of secrets, since you could reveal this secret." Then the king promoted Daniel and gave him many great gifts; and he made him ruler over the whole province of Babylon, and chief administrator over all the wise men of Babylon. Also Daniel petitioned the king, and he set Shadrach, Meshach, and Abed-Nego over the affairs of the province of Babylon; but Daniel sat in the gate of the king.*
> *Daniel 2: 46-49*

Although Daniel was in captivity, he rose to prominence because of the providence of God. No matter where he was, his light had to shine for all men to see God's Glory. The Spirit of God had to locate him in captivity to accomplish God's purpose.

Daniel's enemies became unhappy with his sudden change in status; they had lost their position as the king's eyes and ears, they could not imagine an outsider and foreigner being the king's confidante.

Daniel also served under King Belshazzar, the son of Nebuchadnezzar, and then under King Darius, the third great king of Babylon. King Darius made Daniel one of the three presidents to rule over 120 satraps appointed to govern the kingdom. Daniel distinguished himself and became the king's preferred choice, once again jealously raised its ugly head from the camp of the rulers because they could not match Daniel in conduct, word or faith. Since they could not find fault in his loyalty to the king, they sought to destroy him for his known reverence for God.

These men approached King Darius and asked him to issue a decree lasting for thirty days in which everyone must worship the king. However, Daniel continued as he did before, he worshiped, praised and prayed to God in full view of everyone as his window was open. His enemies reported him to the king expecting Daniel to deny the allegation but he confirmed their report.

The king became bound to throw Daniel into the lions' den but tried to find a way of circumventing the decree he had made. Daniel did not protest but told the king that the God whom he served would vindicate him. A stone was placed over the den and the king went home to pray to God for Daniel's safety. The king fasted throughout the night in sobriety of heart. In the morning, at dawn, the king ran to the den and was shocked to find Daniel alive. What Daniel's enemies thought would happen did not happen. God shut the mouths of the lions and put his enemies to silence. God showed up and delivered him out of the snare that his enemies had planned for him (Daniel 6:15-24).

Psalm 4:1 says that when I call upon the Lord He will answer my righteous call; He will free me from the clutches of my enemies when I am in trouble.

Daniel became a respected adviser to the kings he served. His character took him far; his commitment to God was unquestionable. Although he entered Babylon as a slave he did not have a captive's mentality. He did not allow anything or anyone stop him from fulfilling his purpose in life. He knew who God had created him to be and he became that person; he lived purposefully. You too must seize the moment and make use of every opportunity that comes your way.

SHADRACH, MESHACH AND ABEDNEGO

Shadrach, Meshach and Abednego were taken by King Nebuchadnezzar into captivity to Babylon and trained to be courtiers. The King promoted them along with Daniel to positions of authority. The officials became jealous of these men because they had taken key positions in the kings' reshuffled government.

Their enemies found an opportunity to discredit them from their positions when the king caused a golden image of himself to be erected. The King had pronounced that every man must bow to the image when they heard the sound of the instruments playing. As these men refused to worship the image of the King, their enemies went to the king to report that they had refused to comply with the King's enactment.

The king in anger called and questioned them about their disobedience in paying homage to his statute; they were bold to stand before the king to inform him that they would not worship his golden image. The king threatened to throw them in the furnace but they insisted that they would not bow down even if God did not come through for them; they showed grit and character.

Their commitment saw them through their challenges. God Himself came into the midst of the fire; the king saw the appearance of a fourth man who cooled the fire down. Although the heat should have killed them, they suffered no scorching and they came out intact.

> *"Then King Nebuchadnezzar was astonished; and he rose in haste and spoke, saying to his counsellors, "Did we not cast three men bound into the midst of the fire?" They answered and said to the king, "True, O king." "Look!" he answered, "I see four men loose, walking in the midst of the fire; and they are not hurt, and the form of the fourth is like the Son of God" Daniel 3: 24-25 NKJV.*

As a result of what he saw, the king decreed that no one should speak against the God of Shadrach, Meshach and Abednego. If these men were not upright in their hearts, God would not have vindicated them. They stood out in a foreign land and became prominent men in the king's cabinet. What are you doing with the gifting that God has placed in your life?

What do you do when you are challenged? Do you automatically give in or do you stand up for your convictions? As believers, we must not compromise our beliefs or allow others to manipulate or intimidate us into making wrong decisions or taking wrong actions.

THE MEN OF GADARA

Jesus travelled all night to keep His appointment with two men in the country of the Gadarenes who needed Him the most. These men lived in the tombs and they became a terror to the residents of the city. The Bible says that people had kept away from them because of their violent nature. They caused fear in the hearts of the people they came across.

When Jesus arrived to heal them, He noticed that they were out of control. They had lost all sense of reasoning as they wandered through the tomb constantly. As these men had been taken over by satan they were unable to help themselves. Their agony must have reached far across to where Jesus Christ was that He came to town just for them. God had destined these men for greatness but satan had interfered with their destiny.

> *"And when He arrived at the other side in the country of the Gadarenes, two men under the control of demons went to meet Him, coming out of the tombs, so fierce and savage that no one was able to pass that way. And behold, they shrieked and screamed, What have You to do with us, Jesus, Son of God? Have You come to torment us before the appointed time? Now at some distance from there a drove of many hogs was grazing. And the demons begged Him, If You drive us out, send us into the drove of hogs. And He said to them, Be gone! So they came out and went into the hogs, and behold, the whole drove rushed down the steep bank into the sea and died in the water. The herdsmen fled and went into the town and reported everything, including what had happened to the men under the power of demons. And behold, the whole town went out to meet Jesus; and as soon as they saw Him, they begged Him to depart from their locality"*
> *(Matthew 8:28- 34 -Amp).*

When Jesus Christ set these men free, the herdsmen who saw what had happened ran to town to report what Jesus had done. When these men's immediate family and neighbours heard the news of their healing they ran to see for themselves. These men became living testimonies of the goodness of God. They went everywhere preaching the message of healing and restoration. God had ordained these men to be ministers but the devil had sabotaged their destiny by taking hold of their minds.

A similar incident is recorded in Mark 5:1-20, there was a man who continually lived in the tombs, he shrieked so loudly that no one had the strength to restrain him because of the unclean spirit operating within him. After Jesus healed him, the unclean spirit left and he became clothed and in his right mind. This man began to preach and testify in Decapolis (ten cities) about what Jesus Christ had done in his life. Many people gave their lives to God because of his testimony.

Jesus Christ sent these men to preach to their family, neighbours and neighbouring cities. Once you receive your healing, rise up and preach a message of restoration to others who need to hear it.

Any of these men may remind you of yourself because you may have endured sexual, physical, psychological, emotional or mental abuse which has had an adverse impact on your life. The abuse may have negatively shaped your perception of life. It may also have affected your relationship with your family and friends; we want you to know that God will free you of those past entanglements and the bitterness and anger you may still be feeling.

You may feel that there is no way back from the challenges that you have been through, just as God restored these men to their rightful place in Him so likewise God will remove the mental blockage that prevents you from receiving your restoration. The Good News is that once you allow Jesus Christ into your life He would transform your life, refine you and replenish all that you have lost. He will give you a future that you can be proud off. The world will hear about your transformation and see the manifestation of God's Hands upon your life.

THE PARALYTIC MAN

At Capernaum, Jesus saw a man who was paralyzed and prostrated by illness lying on a sleeping pad. The paralytic man had dreams and aspirations but was paralysed by his disability. However, he had good friends in his life who wanted to see him healed. Although there was no room for the paralytic man, his friends made room for him to enter, because they believed that once Jesus saw their friend he would be healed.

"Then they came to Him, bringing a paralytic who was carried by four men. And when they could not come near Him because of the crowd, they uncovered the roof where He was. So when they had broken through, they let down the bed on which the paralytic was lying. When Jesus saw their faith, He said to the paralytic, "Son, your sins are forgiven you" Mark 2:3-5.

Jesus told the paralytic man to pick up his sleeping pad and go to his house. He went home because he ceased to be a burden to his family. He carried his sleeping mat, which he previously did not have the strength to carry. He was no longer a liability to those around him.

LEVI

After Jesus Christ healed the paralytic man, he still had time to restore Levi, son of Alphaesus, the tax collector who was "spiritually and morally sick in the eyes of the Scribes". Jesus Christ went to Levi's house to eat and fellowship with him.

"As he went along, he saw Levi, the son of Alphaeus. He was sitting at the place where people come to pay taxes. Jesus said to him, `Come with me.' Levi stood up and went with him. Jesus was eating in Levi's house. Many tax collectors and bad people also came. They sat down to eat with Jesus and his disciples. There were many who went with him. The scribes and Pharisees saw that Jesus ate with these people. They said to the disciples, `Why does he eat and drink with bad people?' Jesus heard it. He said to them, `People who are

well do not need a doctor. But sick people need him. I did
not come to call good people. I came to call bad people to
stop doing wrong things" (Mark 2: 14-17-NIV).

Some refused to hang around with Levi for fear of being called a "lover of sinners" by their self- righteous brethren. Jesus pointed out to the Pharisees that He came to restore those who were lost. Those who feel they have already arrived at their destination are of no use to Him.

THE INFIRMED WOMAN OF EIGHTEEN YEARS

This woman was in the Synagogue on the Sabbath when Jesus Christ saw her. She was bent over and was unable to strengthen herself up as she had been bound for the past eighteen years of her life, she may have lost hope of ever being healed. Despite the large crowd in the Synagogue, Jesus Christ's spirit was drawn to her and He noticed her, He saw her and had compassion on her. The Pharisees and Elders of the Synagogue were not happy when Jesus called her forward to Himself to release her from the bondage of her past. They were more concerned about their rigid order of service.

It appeared that this woman's infirmity had suited them, she was their reference point every Sabbath. They were not ashamed that they were spiritually dead and had not been able to heal her. Yet when Jesus healed her, they were jealous because He showed up their spiritual indifference and intolerance.

'Now He was teaching in one of the synagogues on the
Sabbath. And behold, there was a woman who had a
spirit of infirmity eighteen years, and was bent over and
could in no way raise herself up. But when Jesus saw her,
He called her to Him and said to her, "Woman, you are
loosed from your infirmity." And He laid His hands on her,
and immediately she was made straight, and glorified

> *God. But the ruler of the synagogue answered with indignation, because Jesus had healed on the Sabbath... The Lord then answered him and said, "Hypocrite! Does not each one of you on the Sabbath loose his ox or donkey from the stall, and lead it away to water it? So ought not this woman, being a daughter of Abraham, whom Satan has bound—think of it—for eighteen years, be loosed from this bond on the Sabbath?" ... all the multitude rejoiced for all the glorious things that were done by Him"*
> Luke 13: 10-17.

Jesus Christ called this woman a daughter of Abraham because He knew the covenant relationship that stood between God and Abraham. He saw her as a seed of Abraham who should equally benefit from the covenant of prosperity and healing. He therefore made it His business to heal her of her infirmity.

It took one encounter with Jesus Christ to set this woman free. One encounter with Jesus Christ is all you need for your story to change. Do not give up, as He will surely loosen you from the strongholds of the past.

THE BLIND MAN AT THE ROADSIDE OF JERICHO

When this blind man heard that Jesus of Nazareth was passing through the city, he shouted with his might to attract His attention. His persistence caused Jesus to stop and ask him to be brought forward. Jesus asked this man what he could do for him, obviously Jesus could see that the man was blind but He wanted the man to be specific about his request. Not only must you be persistent in your request to God you must also be specific, Jesus responded by healing the man's eyes.

Although there was a crowd of people with Jesus who were hanging around Him, the blind man did not allow their presence to hinder him from shouting out to receive his healing.

"Then it happened, as He was coming near Jericho, that a certain blind man sat by the road begging. And hearing a multitude passing by, he asked what it meant. So they told him that Jesus of Nazareth was passing by. And he cried out, saying, "Jesus, Son of David, have mercy on me!" Then those who went before warned him that he should be quiet; but he cried out all the more, "Son of David, have mercy on me!" So Jesus stood still and commanded him to be brought to Him. And when he had come near, He asked him, saying, "What do you want Me to do for you?" He said, "Lord, that I may receive my sight." Then Jesus said to him, "Receive your sight; your faith has made you well." And immediately he received his sight, and followed Him, glorifying God. And all the people, when they saw it, gave praise to God" Luke 18: 35-43.

ZACCHAEUS, A CHIEF TAX COLLECTOR

Zacchaeus was small in statute but was not small in foresight. When he tried to see Jesus he could not do so because the crowd had blocked his view so he ran ahead of the crowd and climbed up a sycamore tree in order to see Jesus. When Jesus reached the tree, He stopped, looked up and invited Himself to Zacchaeus's house. Zacchaeus stood out because he was a short man, a tax collector and because he took bold actions to obtain what he wanted.

"When Jesus reached the spot, he looked up and said to him, "Zacchaeus, come down immediately. I must stay at your house today." So he came down at once and welcomed him gladly. All the people saw this and began to mutter, "He has gone to be the guest of a 'sinner.' "But Zacchaeus stood up and said to the Lord, "Look, Lord! Here and now I give half of my possessions to the poor, and if I have cheated anybody out of anything, I will pay back four times the amount." Jesus said to him, "Today salvation has come to this house,

because this man, too, is a son of Abraham. For the Son of Man came to seek and to save what was lost" (Luke 19: 5-10-NIV).

When people heard that Jesus Christ was spending the day with their enemy, they voiced their opinions. They felt Jesus should not associate Himself with a tax collector who stole from others. His accusers felt that they were better at judging his moral and spiritual state than Jesus Christ. Zacchaeus had been waiting for his day of redemption, so he stood up and pledged his repentance.

How far are you prepared to run ahead of the crowd and separate yourself in order to see and hear from God? You must hear God's voice clearly if you want to live victoriously!

Zacchaeus' story correlates with that of the criminal crucified on the cross with Jesus Christ. The criminal knew that if he repented before he died he would be saved. He asked Jesus to remember him when He entered His Kingdom. Jesus assured the criminal that he would surely have a place with Him in paradise. The criminal received redemption by his action of faith in believing that Jesus Christ had the power to grant him what he had requested. It did not matter to Jesus that the criminal had wasted his life, by humbling himself before Jesus, the criminal had secured himself eternal life (*Luke 23: 32-43*).

Remember that no matter how far you may seem to be away from Jesus, once you call upon Him to come into your life in true repentance, He will forgive you all your sins and redeem you back to Him.

THE SAMARITAN WOMAN

Jesus Christ approached a woman who had five ex-husbands and was currently living with her lover for a drink of water. The woman was shocked that Jesus being a Jew and a man would consider her worthy to talk to, as Jews never associated with gentiles.

Jesus told her that He would give her water, which would quench her thirst and shall become a spring of water welling up within her leading to eternal life. She was impressed that Jesus knew about her past, she concluded that for Him to associate with her He must be a Prophet. On account of the woman's transformation many Samaritans placed their trust in Jesus because of her testimony, they saw that Jesus had transformed her life from a meaningless survivor to a purposeful believer.

> "And many of the Samaritans of that city believed in Him because of the word of the woman who testified, "He told me all that I ever did." So when the Samaritans had come to Him, they urged Him to stay with them; and He stayed there two days. And many more believed because of His own word. Then they said to the woman, "Now we believe, not because of what you said, for we ourselves have heard Him and we know that this is indeed the Christ, the Savoir of the world." John 4: 39-42.

THE CRIPPLE AT THE POOL

On the Sabbath, Jesus saw a crippled man by the pool near the Sheep Gate in Jerusalem. The man's condition had persisted for thirty-eight years because there was no one to help him reach the pool on time. Jesus asked the man if he wanted His healing. The man said he did, Jesus then told the man to get up, pick up his bed and walk into his destiny. This man became a testimony of God's power and a thorn in the flesh of the Jews. God intended for this man to walk with dignity and therefore he was worthy of Jesus' attention (*John 5*).

THE WOMAN CAUGHT IN ADULTERY

The scribes and Pharisees brought a woman to Jesus and misquoted the scriptures in Deuteronomy 22:22 for their own benefit. They told Jesus that Moses said such a woman like her who was caught in the act of adultery should be stoned to death; they however ignored the fact that it took two to commit the offence. They did not bring the man to Jesus to be stoned; this showed they were not fair but discriminatory in their application of the law.

> *"So when they continued asking Him, He raised Himself up and said to them, "He who is without sin among you, let him throw a stone at her first." And again He stooped down and wrote on the ground. Then those who heard it, being convicted by their conscience, went out one by one, beginning with the oldest even to the last. And Jesus was left alone, and the woman standing in the midst. When Jesus had raised Himself up and saw no one but the woman, He said to her, "Woman, where are those accusers of yours? Has no one condemned you?" She said, "No one, Lord." And Jesus said to her, "Neither do I condemn you; go and sin no more." John 8: 7-11.*

These self-righteous men asked Jesus what sentence He would impose upon her. When they persisted and insisted that He condemn her, Jesus stooped down and wrote on the ground, the men from the eldest to the youngest began backtracking after Jesus Christ said that the man without sin should cast the first stone. Jesus did not condemn the woman but bestowed mercy and His unmerited favour on her, which had a greater impact on her life.

When people make mistakes instead of openly rebuking them, you should graciously pardon them and lead them back on the right path from which they have strayed. No doubt, this woman had committed a sin and had broken a commandment, she was fallible and so are we! Jesus pointed out to the Pharisees that they set themselves up to judge by the flesh and they condemn men by their external and moral standards but He did not come into the world to judge as men did, who condemn others without giving them the chance to repent first.

THE BLIND MAN FROM BIRTH

As Jesus was passing along on the Sabbath He noticed a man who had been born blind, Jesus disciples asked Him whether the man or his parents had sinned to cause his blindness. Jesus responded by explaining to them that the man was born blind so that the purpose of God can be revealed through the man.

Jesus healed the man by spitting on the ground, making clay with His saliva, then rubbing it on the man's eyes, and asking him to wash them in the pool of Siloam. The blind man obeyed and received his sight. The man's healing attracted a lot of attention from the Pharisees who sought to expel him and his parents from the synagogue. He was born blind so that the workings of God can be manifested in his life.

You may ask God why He permitted the man to go through so much pain, shame and rejection! God knew the man's end from the beginning, had the man been born with sight; he may have missed the mark due to spiritual blindness. When his accusers denied the miracle in his life, the blind man stood up and testified of his healing. Although thrown out of the synagogue, he landed in the kingdom of God (*John 9*).

LAZARUS

Lazarus was the brother of Mary and Martha of Bethany. When he was ill, they sent for Jesus to come and heal him; however, Jesus did not arrive there until after Lazarus was dead and buried. Jesus wanted to demonstrate the resurrection power of God through Lazarus and for the Sadducees to see, as they did not believe in the resurrection of the dead.

Jesus told His disciples that Lazarus was asleep and that He would awaken him from this deep sleep. For Mary and Martha, they thought Jesus had come too late to keep their dreams of seeing

Lazarus live to old age. However, on Jesus' calculation, it was the right time for Him to resurrect Lazarus from death.

> *"When Martha heard that Jesus was coming, she went to meet Him,… Martha then said to Jesus, Master, if You had been here, my brother would not have died. And even now I know that whatever You ask from God, He will grant it to You. Jesus said to her, Your brother shall rise again. Martha replied, I know that he will rise again in the resurrection at the last day. Jesus said to her, I am [Myself] the Resurrection and the Life. Whoever believes in (adheres to, trusts in, and relies on) Me, although he may die, yet he shall live; And whoever continues to live and believes in (has faith in, cleaves to, and relies on) Me shall never [actually] die at all. Do you believe this? She said to Him, Yes, Lord, I have believed [I do believe] that You are the Christ (the Messiah, the Anointed One), the Son of God, [even He] Who was to come into the world. [It is for Your coming that the world has waited.]" (John 11:20-27-Amp).*

When Jesus arrived at their place, he went with Martha and Mary to Lazarus' graveside. He told the mourners to take away the stone, Martha protested but Jesus reminded her that the life giving power was in Him. He told Lazarus to come out of the grave. Lazarus' spirit returned and obeyed the voice of the Lord.

Jesus told the mourners who benefited from celebrating the dead to free Lazarus from his burial garments and to let him go. Jesus did not want Lazarus to remain connected with the dead so He told the people to take away the stone. The rolling away of the stone showed a breaking away of every bondage and hindrance that had held Lazarus down and prevented him from taking hold of his future (*John 11:39-44*).

Jesus commanded those who had come to mourn Lazarus to take away the stones blocking his manifestation and restoration. He did what was impossible with man by raising Lazarus back to life. He destroyed every limitation, confinement, hindrance and bondage that had prevented Lazarus from shining forth to manifest God's glory.

You must remove the stones that have blocked your access to God. The stones may have been stacked up for years and have now created barriers that only spiritual bulldozers can break, with the help of the Holy Spirit, the stones would be broken into pieces. These stones could be spiritual, physical, sexual, psychological, mental or emotional abuse, which you might have endured in your life. They may also be stones of bitterness, hatred, anger, jealousy, un-forgiveness or covetousness. These stones may have been made of concrete, which has caused impenetrable barriers in your life, seek God's help in removing them.

When your dreams are dead or appear to be dead, just hand them over to Jesus and see what He would do. The fact that things do not happen at the time that you expect them to does not mean they would never happen. Do not allow these stones to keep dragging you back to your past, come out of the tomb; take off the shackles, grave clothes and grab hold of your future.

> *You must roll away the stones if you want to see significant changes in your life... and if you are to become all that God has intended for you to be.*

STEPHEN

Stephen was a man of grace and wisdom who diligently served the Lord. His works caused those who belonged to the synagogue to resent and despise him. Some men from the Synagogue of the Freedom including the Cyrenians and Alexandrians could not match Stephen's wisdom, intelligence and ability. They were jealous because their followers had left their fold and joined with

Stephen. They stirred up a dissension against him, got him arrested and accused him of blasphemy.

Even unto death, Stephen was still preaching the gospel of Jesus Christ to those who listened to him. He explained how Jesus Christ had come to the world as promised by God and how they had killed Him. He knew that his assignment was to preach the word of God no matter the situation and he seized his moment to be heard for the last time.

> *"When they heard these things they were cut to the heart, and they gnashed at him with their teeth. But he, being full of the Holy Spirit, gazed into heaven and saw the glory of God, and Jesus standing at the right hand of God, and said, "Look! I see the heavens opened and the Son of Man standing at the right hand of God!" Then they cried out with a loud voice, stopped their ears, and ran at him with one accord; and they cast him out of the city and stoned him. And the witnesses laid down their clothes at the feet of a young man named Saul. And they stoned Stephen as he was calling on God and saying, "Lord Jesus, receive my spirit." Acts 7:54-59.*

Stephen filled with the Holy Spirit pierced the hearts of his enemies; in rage they ground their teeth at him. He saw the Heavens open and Jesus Christ standing by the right hand of God, welcoming and beckoning him into His rest. He knew at that stage that he had completed his assignment. Although he may have lived only for a short period, he left his mark on those he came in contact with. He lived a life of significance and left a legacy behind him. Saul who later became Paul was astonished at the courage Stephen showed even at death.

PHILIP

Phillip was a deacon who evangelised throughout the city of Samaria; he performed miracles, restored cripples to health, preached, and converted many to the church, Simon the magician was one of his converts.

An angel of the Lord told Philip to take the road that ran from Jerusalem to Gaza to meet an Ethiopian eunuch, under Candace, the Queen of Ethiopia. There he ministered to the eunuch who was reading from the book of Isaiah, but did not have an understanding of the scriptures. Philip had the gift of interpretation so he explained the meaning of the scriptures to him; Philip later baptised him and continued on his journey.

The Spirit took Philip away to continue his mission. God saw a faithful and committed servant in Philip. The movement of God is not discriminatory; God does not look at a person's position in the church before using him. God did not consult the apostles or elders of the church before He used Philip to spread the gospel into Ethiopia (*Acts 8*).

All that God requires from you is that you are found faithful. Once He sees that you are faithful to Him, He will take you far in life. Are you ready to go the distance?

DORCAS CALLED TABITHA

Dorcas was the only woman referred to as a Disciple in the Bible. The inhabitants of Joppa knew her to be a person abounding in good works, deeds and charity. Would your neighbours describe you as such?

When Dorcas fell sick and died, the people wept because she was irreplaceable. When the other disciples heard that Peter was near Joppa they sent for him and without hesitation he attended to Dorcas because her reputation had preceded her. Peter hurriedly attended to restore her back to life (Acts 9:36-43).

Dorcas' position as the only woman disciple is remarkable and significant to us in modern times; she did not allow sexism in the church to stop her from fulfilling her calling, by her works men recognised her ability, contributions and achievements.

Women must rise up to be counted amongst the elect; they should positively contribute to the furtherance of the gospel and should not allow sexual discrimination to stop them from influencing their world.

CORNELIUS

Cornelius was a gentile centurion and captain of the Italian regiment; he was devoted to serving God together with his household. When God saw his commitment He sent an angel to him confirming that He had noted his prayers and good works; God told him to send for Simon Peter who was staying with Simon the Tanner.

Although Peter was initially reluctant to associate himself with gentiles, God reminded Peter that He had considered Cornelius to be cleansed and washed by the Blood of Jesus Christ and expected Peter to see him that way. God told Peter to change his spiritual dogmatism, which prevented him accepting Cornelius into the Body of Believers.

Peter returned with Cornelius' attendant and preached the good tidings of Jesus Christ. The Holy Spirit descended on Cornelius and his household. Peter did not object to Cornelius and his family being baptised in the name of Jesus Christ. Cornelius chose to align himself with God and was rewarded; his prayer, praise and worship were pleasing to God who chose to use him as an instrument in spreading the gospel to the gentiles (*Acts 10*).

ONESIMUS

In the book of Philemon, we read that Onesimus, a slave had escaped from Philemon, his master in Colosse to Rome where he became a believer and gave his life to Jesus Christ. He later met Paul whom he associated with and served dutifully; however, as a slave, he was the property of Philemon who had a legal right over him.

Although Onesimus was free in the Lord, his past held him hostage. Paul knew what potential resided within Onesimus and he knew that Onesimus would only be able to maximise and utilise his potential if he settled his differences with Philemon and dealt with his past.

Paul also knew that Onesimus would become more useful to him and Philemon as a supporter in the ministry if he returned to Philemon to ask for forgiveness. In obedience, Onesimus returned to Philemon with a letter from Paul asking for pardon for his previous offences.

Despite their different upbringing and background, Paul saw Onesimus as a spiritual son who had a lot to offer in the future; he therefore took the time to deal with the issues that were preventing Onesimus from moving forward.

Onesimus is a testimony to the body of Christ, that no matter where you start out, prayer coupled with determination and hard work can change your destiny. Paul and the brethren saw his true worth and value, not merely as a slave but as an evangelist (Book of Philemon).

God created you to live life fully, don't settle for less. The mediocre and average person has one thing in common namely laziness and inability to see the wider picture. You must open your heart to receive all that God has in store for you just as these men and women did. Their beginnings may have been insignificant but their end was great because they put in the extra effort that was required to change their location, position and station in life. You must do as these men and women did so that you can fulfil God's purpose and calling for your life. You must live a life of purpose and not that of a drifter.

CHAPTER 5

Walking off the Path

(When You Leave The Path God Created You To Take, You Become what God Did Not Create You To Be)

Walking off the path that God has created you to take will result in the abortion of your destiny. Your life is a path; make sure you journey on God's path for your life. God expects you to keep His commandments and laws, which will keep you on the path of righteousness. The choices you make will determine whether or not you reach your destination. Do not walk off your God given path or in the path of the ungodly.

> "The LORD said, "It is because they have forsaken my law, which I set before them; they have not obeyed me or followed my law. Instead, they have followed the stubbornness of their hearts; they have followed the Baals, as their fathers taught them. "Therefore, this is what the LORD Almighty, the God of Israel, says: "See, I will make this people eat bitter food and drink poisoned water. I will scatter them among nations that neither they nor their fathers have known, and I will pursue them with the sword until I have destroyed them." (Jeremiah 9: 13-16-NIV).

There are numerous people in the Bible who walked off the path that God had ordained for them. Some had the opportunity of repenting but because of their pride and arrogance they did not do so. The easiest way to walk off God's path for your life is to ignore or fail to heed His Word to you. The Scriptures gives an array of men and women who failed to heed God's Voice or walk in their God chosen path. Some of these are:

ADAM AND EVE

When God created man He framed man out of His design and it was His intention that man would fit the purpose for which he was made. Man was constituted with all the elements that would enable him to succeed if he placed his trust and reliance in God.

> *"And the Lord God took the man and put him in the Garden of Eden to tend and guard and keep it. And the Lord God commanded the man, (**Adam**) saying, You may freely eat of every tree of the garden; But of the tree of the knowledge of good and evil and blessing and calamity you shall not eat, for in the day that you eat of it you shall surely die.*
> *Genesis 2: 15-17(Amp).*

> *"NOW THE serpent was more subtle and crafty than any living creature of the field which the Lord God had made. And he [Satan] said to the woman, Can it really be that God has said, You shall not eat from every tree of the garden? And the woman said to the serpent, We may eat the fruit from the trees of the garden, Except the fruit from the tree, which is in the middle of the garden. God has said, You shall not eat of it, neither shall you touch it, lest you die" (Genesis 3:1-3-Amp).*

Satan did not approach Adam directly rather he went to Eve in a subtle manner to appeal to her emotions. He twisted God's Word and said to her that can it really be that God has said she shall not eat from every tree of the garden. He made her doubt God's love and planted doubt into her heart, that perhaps God did not truly care enough to give her what she desired to sustain her. Eve began to reason within herself saying that if God truly loved her, He would not qualify what she can have.

God had already told us that He created man in his own image, to be like Him, so how can the serpent tell Eve that she would now be like God. Eve did not either understand who God had created her to be or she had suffered a memory lapse, like many do in times of trials. We sometimes forget what God has said and listen to the small voices within us. When we fail to discover who God has made us to be we become the person we ought not to be.

> "But the Lord God called to Adam and said to him, 'Where are you? He said, I heard the sound of You [walking] in the garden, and I was afraid because I was naked; and I hid myself. And He said, 'Who told you that you were naked? Have you eaten of the tree of which I commanded you that you should not eat? And the man said, The woman whom You gave to be with me—she gave me [fruit] from the tree, and I ate. And the Lord God said to the woman; 'What is this you have done?' And the woman said, The serpent beguiled (cheated, outwitted, and deceived) me, and I ate. (Genesis 3: 9-13 -Amp).

Adam began the blame game and blamed Eve for his shortcomings and disobedience to God. When people make mistakes or commit sin, they find it easier to blame some other person just as Adam did by blaming Eve. It is believed that by shifting responsibility for one's actions this distracts attention from one's weaknesses.

It would have been much better for Adam to have faced up to his mistake and accept responsibility for his actions instead of playing the blame game with God. The serpent's intention was to separate man from God, he knew that God had chosen man as his favourite creation above him. The serpent's (satan, devil) intention is to displace man's relationship with God. As a result of their disobedience God cursed them and all mankind.

Adam and Eve were driven out of the Garden of Eden for their disobedience, contrary to God's original intention for them. Although the consequences of their disobedience remained with man for centuries it was not perpetual as God in His mercy restored man back to his rightful position through Jesus Christ's death on the cross and resurrection.

We must not deceive ourselves and believe that we are infallible as it is easy to be led astray in moments of weaknesses. You must continuously seek God's face and dwell in His presence if you must truly overcome the schemes of the devil.

CAIN

There was sibling rivalry between the two sons of Adam and Eve. Cain, the first-born began to envy Abel's relationship with God. In due course he brought an offering to the Lord and Abel brought the first born of his flock and the fat portion to the Lord. God accepted Abel's offering but rejected Cain's because he (Cain) had no respect or regard for Him. Cain became exceedingly angry, indignant and depressed.

> "But for Cain and his offering He had no respect or regard.
> So Cain was exceedingly angry and indignant, and he looked
> sad and depressed. And the Lord said to Cain, Why are
> you angry? And why do you look sad and depressed and
> dejected? If you do well, will you not be accepted? And if you
> do not do well, sin crouches at your door; its desire is for you,
> but you must master it" (Genesis 4: 5-7-Amp).

God told Cain that if he did well, his offering and gifts would be accepted. He advised Cain to consider his attitude when giving sacrifices as He looked at the inward heart of a man when he brings his offering before Him. Cain refused to listen to God and chose not to build on his strengths instead he focused on his weaknesses and doubted his position and relationship with God.

If you have a weakness that you do not address, it will eventually grow to control and embarrass you in public when you least expect it to. Cain failed to control his jealousy and anger and allowed them to consume his relationship with his brother. He eventually killed Abel in cold blood thinking that God would not find him out.

> *"And [the Lord] said, What have you done? The voice of your brother's blood is crying to Me from the ground. And now you are cursed by reason of the earth, which has opened its mouth to receive your brother's [shed] blood from your hand. When you till the ground, it shall no longer yield to you its strength; you shall be a fugitive and a vagabond on the earth [in perpetual exile, a degraded outcast]. Then Cain said to the Lord, My punishment is greater than I can bear. Behold, You have driven me out this day from the face of the land, and from Your face I will be hidden; and I will be a fugitive and a vagabond and a wanderer on the earth, and whoever finds me will kill me. And the Lord said to him, Therefore, if anyone kills Cain, vengeance shall be taken on him sevenfold. And the Lord set a mark or sign upon Cain, lest anyone finding him should kill him. So Cain went away from the presence of the Lord and dwelt in the land of Nod [wandering], east of Eden. Genesis 4: 10-16 (Amp).*

Despite being a murderer, God showed mercy towards Cain and did not kill him; however, God cursed him as He had done his parents before him. As a result of his actions, Cain became "*a fugitive, a vagabond and a wanderer*" on the face of the earth, God set a mark/sign upon his head so that he would not be found and killed.

The Compact Oxford English Dictionary-3rd Edition and the Free On-line Dictionary defines fugitive, vagabond and wanderer as:

VAGABOND-

- A person without a permanent home who moves from place to place.
- A vagrant; a tramp.
- Aimless, drifting.

WANDER/ A WANDERER-

- To move about without a definite destination or purpose; to move slowly away from a fixed point or place- to lose the mark

- To go astray: wander from the path of righteousness.

- To lose clarity or coherence of thought or expression.

FUGITIVE-

- Running away or fleeing, as from the law; a refugee;

- Given to change or disappearance; perishable;

- Tending to wander; vagabond.

Cain reached rock bottom because he refused to take correction from God. God never intended for man to be cursed but to be blessed. Cain became an aimless wanderer for the rest of his life. He had been created to dominate and control his environment, which he didn't do. Many have murdered or injured others in anger, which has resulted in their incarceration for life. You just need to visit a prison to see this for yourself, often with hindsight they regret their moment of madness.

Master your weaknesses so that your weaknesses don't master you. You must put your flesh in subjection to God's will. If you are prone to anger, temper or rage you need to do something about it, before you become a fugitive, wanderer or vagabond to your family or the state. Don't allow anger to cause havoc in your life before you take action. God has ordained you for greatness, do whatever it takes to live up to God's expectations. It is interesting to note that many have wandered from the path of righteousness; they have simply missed the point as to why God had created them. It is not God's will that you become an 'aimless wanderer' in life.

AARON

Aaron had a prominent role as the first high priest in Israel yet he led a conflicting and inconsistent life. He was chosen by God to act as Moses' mouthpiece. He was the first appointed High Priest of the tribe of Levi who was ordained by God to offer fire and sacrifices on God's altar. He and his son's were ordained by Moses to enter the innermost part of the temple on behalf of the people of Israel.

Despite Aaron's experience of God and the miracles he saw God perform against Pharaoh, he listened to the voice of the multitude and bowed to pressure. He built a graven image in the likeness of a calf when Moses delayed in coming down from the mountain. After building the calf, he called it their god, built an altar before it and encouraged the people to eat and drink in their worship of it. When Moses heard the sound in the camp, he thought it was the sound of war but Joshua said it was the sound of rejoicing. Moses gave Aaron delegated authority to govern the Israelites in his absence, but Aaron couldn't perform as occasion demanded of him. In fear of what the people would do, he allowed himself to be controlled by the majority.

> *"And Moses said to Aaron, "What did this people do to you that you have brought so great a sin upon them?" So Aaron said, "Do not let the anger of my lord become hot. You know the people that they are set on evil. For they said to me, 'Make us gods that shall go before us; as for this Moses, the man who brought us out of the land of Egypt, we do not know what has become of him.' And I said to them, 'Whoever has any gold, let them break it off.' So they gave it to me, and I cast it into the fire, and this calf came out." Now when Moses saw that the people were unrestrained (for Aaron had not restrained them, to their shame among their enemies"*
> *Exodus 32: 21-25.*

It is surprising that Aaron who couldn't be trusted to lead the Israelites would later challenge Moses' authority to rule over the Israelites. He wanted what he did not have the ability for, God saved him from leprosy only because of the mantle of priesthood on his life (*Numbers 12: 1-12*). Moses later went up with Aaron to Mount Hor where he stripped Aaron of his priestly attire, for rebelling against God's instructions, Aaron also died there (*Numbers 20: 22-29*).

NADAB AND ABIHU (THE SONS OF AARON)

In Leviticus 8, God asked Moses to set apart Aaron and his sons for the priesthood. Both Nadab and Abihu were anointed and set apart to offer sacrifices on behalf of the people of Israel. However they forgot their purpose and allowed pride into their hearts by offering strange and unholy fires before God. As a result of their act of defiance, God consumed them with fire and killed them off.

"Then Nadab and Abihu, the sons of Aaron, each took his censer and put fire in it, put incense on it, and offered profane fire before the LORD, which He had not commanded them. So fire went out from the LORD and devoured them, and they died before the LORD. And Moses said to Aaron, "This is what the LORD spoke, saying: 'By those who come near Me I must be regarded as holy; And before all the people I must be glorified.'" So Aaron held his peace" Leviticus 10:1-3

In a short space of time their destiny was terminated by their arrogance and disobedience. Disobedience is deadly; God killed them for failing to have reverence for Him. May disobedience not get in the way of God's work in your life!

THE TEN ELDERS OF ISRAEL

Shammua of the tribe of Reuben, Shaphat of the tribe of Simeon, Igal of the tribe of Issachar, Palti of the tribe of Benjamin, Gaddiel of the tribe of Zebulun, Gaddi of the tribe of Joseph-Manasseh, Ammiel of the tribe of Dan, Sethur of the tribe of Asher and Nahbi of the tribe of Naphtali were amongst the twelve elders of Israel sent by Moses to spy out the land of Canaan. Their position amongst their people signified strength and power but they were lacking in spiritual insight and discernment.

These men were chosen as the leaders of their tribes because they were expected to do great exploits for the advancement of Israel into the Promised Land. You would expect them therefore to be prayer warriors who would have received a personal revelation of what God had intended for each of them and as a group, however their conduct and response when they returned from spying the promised land showed their level of spiritual maturity (*Numbers 13 and 14*).

> "But the men who had gone up with him said, "We are not able to go up against the people, for they are stronger than we." And they gave the children of Israel a bad report of the land which they had spied out, saying, "The land through which we have gone as spies is a land that devours its inhabitants, and all the people whom we saw in it are men of great stature. There we saw the giants (the descendants of Anak came from the giants); and we were like grasshoppers in our own sight, and so we were in their sight." Number 13:31-33.

When these men went to spy out Canaan they brought back clusters of grapes, pomegranates and figs which they had found. It was hoped that the fruits and abundance of blessings in their possession signified their victory in the spiritual realm; instead they allowed the abundance to reflect their unworthiness of the abundant blessings God was bestowing on them. They forgot all the miracles that they had seen God perform since their departure from Egypt.

They allowed the size of the inhabitants of the land to cloud their judgment. By their conduct and words they discouraged the multitude from taking possession of the Promised Land. Even when Joshua and Caleb tried to persuade them that it was still possible to take possession of the blessings which they had seen with their eyes, they allowed their majority voice to prevail over the positive words of the minority, leading to wailing in the camp.

These elders saw themselves as grasshoppers in their own sights; this is what psychologist calls the grasshopper complex or mentality. Having a low self-esteem is one thing but having a grasshopper complex is another problem altogether. These leaders had a poor perception of God and of themselves. They thought that the giants were thinking that they were grasshoppers; their thinking emanated from their own mindset because they had seen themselves in that light. They felt inferior in statute and in status to the sons of Anak who were reputed to be men of courage; they had obviously left their God out of the equation.

Due to their lack of discernment, foresight and understanding, the forty days they spent spying out the land of Canaan became forty years of wandering for the children of Israel. Their actions led not only to the forfeiture of their own destinies but also those who agreed with their evil report as God killed them all with a plaque.

> *When you feel inadequate, unprepared or ill equipped to carry out the tasks God has assigned to you, you should stop and remember that if He has selected and nominated you then He will surely equip, empower and make you capable of fulfilling your assignment.*

When you go against God you are likely to suffer adverse consequences for your disobedience. By bringing back an adverse report these men were saying that God was not capable of fulfilling His side of the bargain and that His Power and might was not above the situation they were facing. Whatever challenges you may encounter, our prayer is that you would hear the voice of God when He speaks. The greater the spiritual position you hold the more accountable you become.

THE REBELS

Korah, Dathan and Abiram rose up with On, 150 princes and some elders of Israel against Moses and Aaron. These three men felt that they were as good as Moses and should be accredited with the same status and pre-eminence as him so they gathered a group of supporters to champion their course.

Korah was a Levite who had a significant spiritual role but he was not satisfied with his appointment, it appeared he wanted the priesthood as well. These three men formed an alliance to take over the leadership from Moses. Leadership rivalry is not only an occurrence of the twenty first century; it has been in existence from the beginning of the early church. To worsen their situation, when Moses called them to a meeting to settle the dispute they refused to attend.

These three elders were filled with their own self-importance; they erroneously believed that God would disregard the mantle He had placed on Moses for them. Their jealousy and covetousness of Moses' and Aaron's calling became apparent as they could no longer curtail their resentment.

> *"They gathered together against Moses and Aaron, and said to them, "You take too much upon yourselves, for all the congregation is holy, every one of them, and the LORD is among them. Why then do you exalt yourselves above the assembly of the LORD?" Numbers: 16:3.*

These men manifested what was in their hearts. They forgot that Moses did not get to his position by his own strength; he was not a shooting star but had received his training and ordination in the wilderness. Because they set the congregation against Moses, God killed them by opening up the ground and consuming them and their families. Fire also consumed the 250 followers who had set up and offered incense to God, which they were not qualified to offer.

> *"And Moses said: "By this you shall know that the LORD has sent me to do all these works, for I have not done them of my own will. If these men die naturally like all men, or if they are visited by the common fate of all men, then the LORD has not sent me. But if the LORD creates a new thing, and the earth opens its mouth and swallows them up with all that belongs to them, and they go down alive into the pit, then... as he finished speaking all these words, that the ground split apart under them, and the earth opened its mouth and swallowed them up, with their households and all the men with Korah, with all their goods. So they and all those with them went down alive into the pit; the earth closed over them, and they perished from among the assembly" (Numbers 16: 28-33).*

These men started well but lost their focus, God intended for them to be helpers to Moses but instead they wanted to usurp his authority and promote themselves prematurely resulting in their destiny being aborted. When God feels that you are ready to be promoted He will promote you.

You must learn not to run ahead of God but to wait for His timing and promotion. Although you may not like your current position it is not a good reason for you to covet and/or revolt against those whom God has placed in charge of you.

SAMSON

Before Samson's birth an Angel of the Lord appeared to his barren mother, the wife of Manoah to pronounce that she would have a son who would be a Nazrite to God. It was foretold that Samson would free his people from the hands of the Philistines who had dominated them.

When Samson grew up, he went to Timnah and saw one of the daughters of the Philistines whom he wanted as a wife. His parents tried to dissuade him and suggested that he marry one of their own, he refused. Samson had begun to breed disobedience in his heart; however, the hand of God was upon him.

On one occasion, Samson's parents went with him to the vineyards of Timnah, on his way Samson killed a lion with his bare hands and on his way back he stopped to look at the lion. He took honey from inside the dead lion, ate and gave his parents some to eat without telling them where it came from.

Samson gave a riddle to the Philistines to solve and asked them to provide an answer to him within seven days. However they persuaded his wife to entice him into revealing the answer. In anger, Samson went down to Ashkelon and slew thirty men and took their garments, which he gave to the men who had answered his riddle. In revenge Samson's wife was given to his best friend.

He later returned to reconcile with his wife but was prevented from doing so by her father. In annoyance he torched the tails of foxes and caused them to pass through the fields of the Philistines. The Philistines responded by killing Samson's wife and her father causing war between Israel and the Philistines. Samson later went down to Gaza where he saw a harlot and went into her. When the Gazities heard of it they planned to kill him but he fled during the night.

Samson met Delilah, who lived in the valley of Sorek, once again the Philistines were told and they persuaded Delilah to entice Samson to find out the secret of his strength. Samson had a weakness for foreign women who did not share the same spiritual and moral values as he did. Samson also had no control over his sexual appetite, which led to his failure to live as a Nazarite.

'And it came to pass, when she pestered him daily with her words and pressed him, so that his soul was vexed to death, that he told her all his heart, and said to her, "No razor has ever come upon my head, for I have been a Nazirite to God from my mother's womb. If I am shaven, then my strength will leave me, and I shall become weak, and be like any other man." When Delilah saw that he had told her all his heart, she sent and called for the lords of the Philistines ... Then she lulled him to sleep on her knees, and called for a man and had him shave off the seven locks of his head. Then she began to torment him, and his strength left him. And she said, "The Philistines are upon you, Samson!" So he awoke from his sleep, and said, "I will go out as before, at other times, and shake myself free!" But he did not know that the LORD had departed from him. Then the Philistines took him and put out his eyes" Judges 16:16-21.

God had great plans for Samson but Samson wanted to fulfil his own desires. He was tall, handsome and gloried in his long hair; eventually it was his long hair that led to his downfall. Samson had broken all the rules laid down by God. He was arrested and enslaved, while being used to entertain the Philistine elite; he pushed the pillars upon which the house rested, killing along with himself, both men and women including Princes of Philistine. Although he repented, he died prematurely.

HOPHNI AND PHINEHAS (THE SONS OF ELI)

Hophni and Phinehas, the sons of Eli were the Priests during the time Hannah brought Samuel to Eli to nurture. They were notoriously greedy and gluttonous; they disregarded the sanctity of the temple and the sacrifices that were offered on the altar. They sent their servants to take the best portion of the sacrifices when they were being cooked and demanded raw meat from the people and refused to allow them to burn the fat as incense to God.

During this time Samuel began to minister to the Lord who preferred him over Hophini and Phinehas. Eli cautioned his children but they ignored his advice. They began to have sexual intercourse with the women who served at the door of the tent of temple so that they became an abomination to God. God sent a prophet to Eli to inform him that the priesthood had been taken away from his family.

"A man of God came to Eli and said to him, Thus has the Lord said: I plainly revealed Myself to the house of your father [forefather Aaron] when they were in Egypt in bondage to Pharaoh's house. Moreover, I selected him out of all the tribes of Israel to be My priest, to offer on My altar, to burn incense, to wear an ephod before Me… Why then do you kick [trample upon, treat with contempt] My sacrifice and My offering which I commanded, and honour your sons above Me by fattening yourselves upon the choicest part of every offering of My people Israel? … Behold, the time is coming when I will cut off your strength and the strength of your own father's house, that there shall not be an old man in your house. And you shall behold the distress of My house, even in all the prosperity, which God will give Israel, and there shall not be an old man in your house forever… And what befalls your two sons, Hophni and Phinehas, shall be a sign to you—in one day they both shall die. [Fulfilled in I Sam. 4:17, 18.] And I will raise up for Myself a faithful priest (Priest), who shall do according to what is in My heart and mind. And I will build him a sure house, and he shall walk before My anointed (Anointed) forever. Everyone who is left in your house shall come crouching to him for a piece of silver and a bit of bread and say, Put me, I pray you, into a priest's office so I may have a piece of bread" (1 Samuel 2: 27-36-Amp).

When the sons of Eli went up with the Ark of Covenant to fight against the Philistines Israel was defeated. They were killed and the

Ark of covenant was taken. Eli was ninety-eight years old when he heard the report; he fell backwards and died from shock and grief. When Phinehas' wife heard the news she went into labour and gave birth to a son whom she called 'ICHABOD' meaning "the glory of The Lord had departed from Israel this day", she later died that day.

Anyone who is opposed to God's Purity, Holiness or Sanctity is clearly an enemy of God. Eli and his sons tore the Priesthood away from their family by their actions. God pronounced a generational curse on Eli and his household that they would all die young in their family (*1 Samuel 3: 12-14*).

Our prayer is that we would not allow our actions destroy all that God has planned for us.

JOEL AND ABIJAH (THE SONS OF SAMUEL)

Joel and Abijah were sons of Prophet Samuel; they lived abhorrent lives before the Lord, just as the sons of Eli did. Samuel appointed his sons as judges over Israel but instead of them settling disputes and dealing justly with the people they resorted to taking bribes and perverting the course of justice so that the people rose up against them in protest and demanded that Samuel appoint a King over them.

> *"When Samuel grew old, he appointed his sons as judges*
> *for Israel. The name of his firstborn was Joel and the name*
> *of his second was Abijah, and they served at Beersheba.*
> *But his sons did not walk in his ways. They turned aside*
> *after dishonest gain and accepted bribes and perverted*
> *justice. So all the elders of Israel gathered together and*
> *came to Samuel at Ramah. They said to him, "You are*
> *old, and your sons do not walk in your ways; now appoint*
> *a king to lead us, such as all the other nations have."*
> *1 Samuel 8:2-4 (NIV).*

It is appalling that Samuel like Aaron and Eli could not control his children despite his position and commitment to God; Joel and Abijah did not have the same zeal and reverence as their father had. However unlike Eli who was punished for his sons' sins, God did not punish Samuel for the transgression of his wayward sons.

SAUL

When Saul was looking for his father's lost donkeys, his servant advised him to seek Samuel's assistance in finding them. On their way, God spoke to Samuel in advance to anoint Saul as king as he was chosen to rule the people of Israel. Samuel anointed Saul as king and later confirmed Saul as king in the presence of all the Israelites

Saul, a Benjamite, was appointed the first king of Israel when the Israelites were displeased about judges ruling over them. He was tall and more handsome than any other man of his time. He was forty years old when he began his reign; his first assignment was to fight against Nahash the Ammonite whom he conquered as God gave him victory.

Samuel later told Saul to meet him at Gilgal to renew Saul's kingship as the people's choice, however while waiting for Samuel for seven days the Philistines assembled to fight against the Israelites. In fear Saul decided to offer both burnt and peace offerings in disobedience to God as he did not like to lose face in front of his subjects, just as he completed the sacrifices Samuel appeared.

> 'Now it happened, as soon as he had finished presenting the burnt offering that Samuel came; and Saul went out to meet him, that he might greet him. And Samuel said, "What have you done?" Saul said, "When I saw that the people were scattered from me, and that you did not come within the

*days appointed, and that the Philistines gathered together
at Michmash, then I said, 'The Philistines will now come
down on me at Gilgal, and I have not made supplication to
the LORD.' Therefore I felt compelled, and offered a burnt
offering." And Samuel said to Saul, "You have done foolishly.
You have not kept the commandment of the LORD your
God, which He commanded you. For now the LORD would
have established your kingdom over Israel forever. But now
your kingdom shall not continue. The LORD has sought
for Himself a man after His own heart, and the LORD has
commanded him to be commander over His people, because
you have not kept what the LORD commanded you" 1
Samuel 13:10-14.*

Saul found an excuse for his disobedience when challenged but God saw through them. Samuel told him that his reign would not continue and that God had appointed another person in his place. Saul wanted to feel important in the sight of his subjects but instead of his elevation he was demoted.

On another occasion, Samuel told Saul that he was to go out and defeat the Amalekites for what they did to the Israelites when they came out of Egypt. Saul was told to destroy everything that the Amalekites owned including the people and their animals. Although he killed the people, he spared Agag, king of the Amelikites and the best of the animals. God told Samuel that he had repented the day Saul was made king. Samuel rebuked Saul but again he tried to make excuses for his disobedience by apportioning the blame on his subjects.

*"Samuel said, Has the Lord as great a delight in burnt
offerings and sacrifices as in obeying the voice of the
Lord? Behold, to obey is better than sacrifice, and to
hearken than the fat of rams. For rebellion is as the sin of
witchcraft, and stubbornness is as idolatry and teraphim
(household good luck images). Because you have rejected
the word of the Lord, He also has rejected you from being*

king. And Saul said to Samuel, I have sinned; for I have transgressed the commandment of the Lord and your words, because I feared the people and obeyed their voice. Now, I pray you, pardon my sin and go back with me, that I may worship the Lord. And Samuel said to Saul, I will not return with you; for you have rejected the word of the Lord, and the Lord has rejected you from being king over Israel. And as Samuel turned to go away, Saul seized the skirt of Samuel's mantle, and it tore. And Samuel said to him, The Lord has torn the kingdom of Israel from you this day and has given it to a neighbour of yours who is better than you" (1 Samuel 15: 22-28-Amp).

God told Samuel that he had regretted making Saul, king. Samuel shook his hands off Saul and never saw Saul until his death. Saul had with his own hands ripped the kingdom away from himself; he did not need any enemy to do that for him.

May God never regret the day that He promoted us! There are people who continue to sin and when confronted they blame others for their crooked character. There are abusers who would rather blame their victims for their weaknesses and shortcomings instead of owning up to their faults. The good news is that God cannot be mocked for whatsoever a man sows, he shall reap.

Shortly afterwards God anointed David as king in place of Saul. The Lord departed from Saul and an evil spirit began to torment him. David was called to minister to Saul to calm him down; however Saul began to hate David because he was more popular than he was with the people. When David gained victory over the Philistines and killed Goliath, the women sang in his honour causing Saul to despise David further.

Saul tried to kill David and cursed his son Jonathan for assisting him. He killed Ahimelech, the priest for assisting David. He subsequently consulted a medium to bring up the ghost of Samuel to reveal what would happen if he went up to fight the Philistines at Gilboa because God had refused to answer his prayers. Saul and his sons later died in the battle at mount Gilboa.

AHITHOPHEL THE GILONITE

Ahithophel was David's counsellor whose advice was followed to the letter. He was one of David's inner circles and was highly respected in Israel. When David was told that Ahithophel had joined the conspiracy with Absalom to overthrow him, David shook with dread because he knew Ahithophel's ability.

Being intelligent and having ability is one thing but being filled with God's wisdom and discernment is another. David asked God to frustrate the mind, wisdom and advice of Ahithophel. He asked Hushai, the Archite to return to the city and join Absalom so that he could frustrate Ahithophel's counsel.

> 'Then someone told David, saying, "Ahithophel is among the conspirators with Absalom." And David said, "O LORD, I pray, turn the counsel of Ahithophel into foolishness!" 2 Samuel 15:31.

Ahithophel advised Absalom to sleep with David's concubines in public so that Israel would know that that Absalom was abhorred by his father and to encourage his supporters in carrying out his revolt for him. Because of David's prayer, God frustrated Ahithopel's counsel to Absalom.

Absalom refused to follow Ahithophel's military strategy but followed the advice given by Hushai as he believed it was better, for God had ordained it that way. When Ahithophel realised that his counsel was not followed, he saddled his donkey, went home to put his house in order and then hung himself and died.

Ahithophel, an old wise man who had been greatly revered and respected by the king and nobles had a humiliating end. He had started well but lost his way in the end (2 Samuel 17).

SOLOMON

Solomon, son of King David and Bathsheba was anointed King over Israel and Judah by Zadok the priest and Nathan the prophet to sit on the throne of his father.

Solomon established his kingdom by ridding himself of those who had been a thorn in his father's flesh as they were also a potential threat to his reign. He killed Adonijah for wanting to usurp his authority; Joab for shedding innocent blood, Shimei for cursing King David (2 Samuel 16:5-6) and expelled Abiathar, the priest from office for conniving to make his brother, Adonijah king over Israel.

> *"And Solomon said…. Now, O LORD my God, You have made Your servant king instead of my father David, but I am a little child; I do not know how to go out or come in. And Your servant is in the midst of Your people whom You have chosen, a great people, too numerous to be numbered or counted. Therefore give to Your servant an understanding heart to judge Your people, that I may discern between good and evil….... Then God said to him: "Because you have asked this thing, and have not asked long life for yourself, nor have asked riches for yourself, nor have asked the life of your enemies, but have asked for yourself understanding to discern justice, behold, I have done according to your words; see, I have given you a wise and understanding heart, so that there has not been anyone like you before you, nor shall any like you arise after you" 1 Kings 3: 6-12.*

At the beginning of his reign Solomon asked God for wisdom to rule his people as he was full of promise- he was faithful, diligent and committed in the things concerning God. He applied wisdom in building the House of the Lord which he began to build in his fourth year. After its completion he dedicated the Temple and brought the Ark of Covenant to rest inside it. He praised and thanked God for qualifying him to build the magnificent Temple in honour of His Name.

Although King Solomon was called a wise man, as there was none who equalled him in wisdom, knowledge, skills and ability, he was still flawed in certain areas of his life. He allowed wealth, prestige and power to cloud his judgement. He took many wives and concubines who led him to worship idols; he forgot the ordinances that Moses gave to the people, one of which said that the King of Israel must not multiply wives to himself. He forgot that God had chosen to elevate him above his brother, Adonijah who was the rightful heir to the throne and he had abused that privilege.

> *"So the LORD said to Solomon, "Since this is your attitude and you have not kept my covenant and my decrees, which I commanded you, I will most certainly tear the kingdom away from you and give it to one of your subordinates. Nevertheless, for the sake of David your father, I will not do it during your lifetime. I will tear it out of the hand of your son. Yet I will not tear the whole kingdom from him, but will give him one tribe for the sake of David my servant and for the sake of Jerusalem, which I have chosen." 1 Kings 11: 11-13 (NIV).*

Solomon's wealth became a snare to him and he lived a life of excess, his lack of discernment and discretion led to God swearing to tear the kingdom out of his descendant's hand. This prophecy was fulfilled when God tore ten tribes of Israel out of Rehoboam's hands and left him with one tribe due to the unbreakable covenant that stood between Him and David, unlike David, his father, Solomon never truly repented of his disobedience.

THE YOUNG PROPHET

There was a young man of God who appeared out of Judah at Bethel to prophesy to Jeroboam as he stood by the altar to burn incense. God sent the young prophet on assignment and was strictly told not to eat anything or return by the way he had come. After completing his assignment the young prophet met an old Prophet who lied to him. The old Prophet gave him a false prophecy resulting in him disobeying God. God now sent the old prophet to tell him that he would die a painful death for his disobedience.

> "The man of God said, "I cannot turn back and go with you, nor can I eat bread or drink water with you in this place. I have been told by the word of the LORD: 'You must not eat bread or drink water there or return by the way you came.' "The old prophet answered, "I too am a prophet, as you are. And an angel said to me by the word of the LORD: 'Bring him back with you to your house so that he may eat bread and drink water.' " (But he was lying to him.) So the man of God returned with him and ate and drank in his house. While they were sitting at the table, the word of the LORD came to the old prophet who had brought him back. He cried out to the man of God who had come from Judah, "This is what the LORD says: 'You have defied the word of the LORD and have not kept the command the LORD your God gave you. You came back and ate bread and drank water in the place where he told you not to eat or drink. Therefore your body will not be buried in the tomb of your fathers" (1 Kings 13: 16-22-NIV).

You must not allow men who appear to be holy and pious to deceive and lead you astray. You must ask God for a discerning spirit so that you can discern which spirit is operating within them so that you do not walk off the path in ignorance. The young prophet had potential but was swayed by the outward appearance of the older prophet.

REHOBOAM

Rehoboam's life mirrors that of the young prophet. When he took over the kingship from his father- Solomon, he relied upon the unwise and foolish counsel of his young male friends instead of the advice of the old men who had once served his father. The advice of his young friends seemed good to him but led to his destruction and the tearing away of ten tribes from his kingdom (2 Chronicles 10).

The word of the Lord never fails; King Solomon's son suffered the consequences of his pride and disobedience. Our decisions can affect our offspring. We need to be careful of our actions as they may bind the future of our children negatively.

AHAB

King Ahab, the son of Omri reigned under the influence of his wife Jezebel, the daughter of Ethbaal, King of Sidon. Due to his wife's dominance and control over his life Israel Ahab took the worship of Baal to a level that was never seen before in Israel. He was reduced to a puppet by his wife.

Ahab's downfall became eminent when he cried to Jezebel over the vineyard that belonged to Naboth, the Jezrelite who refused to sell his inheritance to him; Jezebel ordered for false accusations to be brought against Naboth that he had blasphemed against God. Naboth was killed so that Ahab could take possession of his vineyard (*1 Kings 21 & 22*). God sent Prophet Elijah to tell him that dogs would lick his blood the same way they had licked Naboth's. God also said that dogs would eat Jezebel's body by the wall of Jezreel.

Ahab repented of his sins and for this the Lord promised not to bring evil to him during his lifetime but that evil will be brought during his sons' lifetime. God however swore to cut off every male child in his household. He later died in battle and dogs licked his blood according to God's word.

Ahab lived and died without any remarkable achievements been recorded against his name.

GEHAZI

Gehazi's life exemplifies what happens when a person is motivated by greed. His weaknesses could be seen early on in his relationship with Elisha who had sent him to the Shunammite woman's house to raise her dead son but he could not accomplish this task. On that occasion Elisha had to attend himself to restore the woman's son to life. Gehazi never really reflected upon where he had gone wrong and how he could increase his faith, instead he was interested in being the right hand man of Elisha; he saw his position as a status symbol. With his unique position he should have been preparing himself to take over the mantle from Elisha just as his master had done with Elijah.

When Elisha healed Naaman, a commander in the Syrian army he refused the prophets offering because he saw it as an opportunity to minister to him. However Gehazi could not believe that his master had declined a handsome reward so he ran after Naaman and lied to him that Elisha had changed his mind and wanted the gift. He then hid the gift in his house thinking that Elisha would not discover the folly of his heart. In Holy anger, Elisha rebuked Gehazi for his deceit and cursed him by bringing the leprosy that left Naaman on him.

> *"Go in peace," Elisha said. After Naaman had travelled some distance, Gehazi, the servant of Elisha the man of God, said to himself, "My master was too easy on Naaman, this Aramean, by not accepting from him what he brought. As surely as the LORD lives, I will run after him and get something from him." So Gehazi hurried after Naaman. When Naaman saw him running toward him, he got down from the chariot to meet him. "Is everything all right?" he asked. "Everything is all right," Gehazi answered. "My master sent me... When Gehazi came to the hill, he took the things from the servants and put them away in the house. He sent the men away and they left. Then he went in and stood*

before his master Elisha. "Where have you been, Gehazi?"
Elisha asked. "Your servant didn't go anywhere," Gehazi
answered. But Elisha said to him, "Was not my spirit with
you when the man got down from his chariot to meet you? Is
this the time to take money, or to accept clothes, olive groves,
vineyards, flocks, herds, or menservants and maidservants?
Naaman's leprosy will cling to you and to your descendants
forever." Then Gehazi went from Elisha's presence and he was
leprous, as white as snow 2 Kings 5: 19-27 (NIV).

Although Gehazi had great potential in him he did not learn how to control his covetousness. He was the ideal candidate to take over the mantle from Elisha but he concentrated on his immediate needs and not the long-term benefit of having Elisha as a mentor. He had noticed the gifts and presents that Elisha was receiving and he wanted that which he had not earned or worked for.

HEZEKIAH

Hezekiah, the son of Ahaz, king of Judah began his reign at the age of 25 years and he ruled for 29 years. He determined in his heart not to follow the path of his ancestors but to serve God wholeheartedly and was rewarded for breaking down the idols and removing the high places where the people attended to sacrifice to Baal.

Years later when Hezekiah became ill God told him to put his house in order as he was going to die, Hezekiah prayed to God to spare his life and his prayers were answered.

"In those days Hezekiah became ill and was at the point of
death. The prophet Isaiah son of Amoz went to him and said,
"This is what the LORD says: Put your house in order, because
you are going to die; you will not recover." Hezekiah turned
his face to the wall and prayed to the LORD, "Remember,
O LORD, how I have walked before you faithfully and with

wholehearted devotion and have done what is good in your eyes." And Hezekiah wept bitterly. Before Isaiah had left the middle court, the word of the LORD came to him: "Go back and tell Hezekiah, the leader of my people, 'This is what the LORD, the God of your father David, says: I have heard your prayer and seen your tears; I will heal you. On the third day from now you will go up to the temple of the LORD. I will add fifteen years to your life. And I will deliver you and this city from the hand of the king of Assyria. I will defend this city for my sake and for the sake of my servant David." 2 kings 20: 1-6 (NIV)

Unfortunately Hezekiah did not live out the rest of his life the way that he began, instead of putting his house in order; he began to rejoice in his wealth. He showed the King of Babylon what he had amassed throughout his reign and the wealth that had been stored up by previous kings. Isaiah, the prophet returned to Hezekiah and rebuked him for his act of folly and told him that disaster would befall his descendants.

God must have known that Hezekiah did not have the capacity to continue as he had done before his illness but granted Hezekiah his hearts request so that he would realise that having a short fulfilled life was better than a prolonged one without God (2 kings 20:13-19).

You must think of the consequences of your choices and be cautious of the prayers you utter to God in times of despair. You must not make irrational promises, decisions or choices that may lead to negative consequence for you

> *As God's purpose for our life is sometimes different from ours, we must pray for God's enlightenment and discernment so that we don't miss the mark.*

JUDAS ISCARIOT

Judas which means, "praise" in the bible is now a name that is synonymous with the words "Traitor, Betrayer". When a person is said to be a "Judas", it means that they are a betrayer of confidence. Judas' character is revealed when a woman came up to Jesus with an alabaster flask of precious perfume and poured it over Jesus Christ's head, the disciples notably Judas was furious, angry and livid with the woman for wasting such an expensive oil on Jesus when she could have used the money for something better.

To Jesus this woman had done a noble thing, worthy of His recognition and praise, her act of total worship put her name in the Book of Life. Jesus saw her heart and how earnest she was in washing His feet with her tears and drying His feet with her hair this however was lost on Judas who was motivated by greed. Judas could not understand what had made the woman spend all her earnings on a single gift for Jesus.

Judas was not concerned with the reasons behind the woman's actions. His behaviour revealed his character flaw in that he could not stand another being blessed; he could not stand another person being the focus of Jesus' attention. He forgot that by being part of the twelve apostles, he occupied a unique position.

Judas being discontented with Jesus Christ decided to sell Him for thirty pieces of silver. Judas led the chief priests and elders of Israel to Jesus whilst He was praying in the Garden of Gethsemane and gave Him a kiss to seal his betrayal. Judas was waiting to explode all along and when the opportunity arose; he took it (Matthew 26: 7-16).

> "And while He was still speaking, behold, Judas, one of the twelve, with a great multitude with swords and clubs, came from the chief priests and elders of the people. Now His betrayer had given them a sign, saying, 'Whomever I kiss, He

*is the One; seize Him.' Immediately he went up to Jesus and
said, 'Greetings, Rabbi!' and kissed Him. But Jesus said to
him, 'Friend, why have you come?' Then they came and laid
hands on Jesus and took Him" Mt. 26: 47-50.*

Judas Iscariot did not show true repentance for betraying
Jesus Christ, instead of approaching Jesus Christ after His resur-
rection to plead for forgiveness,
Judas took the easy way out and
hung himself. We are persuaded that
Jesus Christ would have forgiven
him if he had asked Him to
(Matthew 27:3-5-NKJV).

> *There is no use having
> a purpose that does not
> benefit those around you,
> when you leave this earth
> how do you want people
> to remember you?*

It could be argued that Judas's
betrayal had been predestined so he
had no free choice in the matter. After all Jesus Christ appointed
the Twelve Disciples knowing that one of them would betray
him! (John 6:70), even the Old Testament had foretold it. Judas
will forever be remembered for his betrayal and bigotry. Where
there is no vision or fresh revelation from God, stagnation persists
(Proverbs 29:18).

ANANIAS AND SAPPHIRA

At a time when the believers were growing in number, the wealthy
amongst them including Barnabas sold their lands or houses and
brought in turn their proceeds to the Apostles for the benefit of the
needy, destitute and poor.

When Ananias and Sapphira saw this they decided to follow
the believers' example. They sold their piece of land and decided to
hold back some of the money they received. Ananias then brought
some of the proceeds to Peter lying about the amount he had
received, Peter saw the deceit and confronted Ananias about his
deceitfulness, and he was struck down and killed.

Sapphira not realising what had happened repeated the same lie to Peter who told her that the same men who had gone to bury her husband were waiting for her; she too dropped dead at the feet of Peter.

> "But Peter said, Ananias, why has Satan filled your heart
> that you should lie to and attempt to deceive the Holy
> Spirit, and should [in violation of your promise] withdraw
> secretly and appropriate to your own use part of the price
> from the sale of the land? As long as it remained unsold,
> was it not still your own? And [even] after it was sold, was
> not [the money] at your disposal and under your control?
> Why then, is it that you have proposed and purposed in
> your heart to do this thing? [How could you have the heart
> to do such a deed?] You have not [simply] lied to men
> [playing false and showing yourself utterly deceitful] but
> to God. Upon hearing these words, Ananias fell down and
> died... Now after an interval of about three hours his wife
> came in, not having learned of what had happened. And
> Peter said to her, Tell me, did you sell the land for so much?
> Yes, she said, for so much. Then Peter said to her, How
> could you two have agreed and conspired together to try to
> deceive the Spirit of the Lord? Listen! The feet of those who
> have buried your husband are at the door, and they will
> carry you out [also]. And instantly she fell down at his feet
> and died; and the young men entering found her dead, and
> they carried her out and buried her beside her husband."
> (Acts 5:3-10).

Competing with others is costly; some have a competitive and covetous spirit and are always seeking to outperform or outdo others. This attitude is dangerous. Trying to compete with others by giving a pledge or vow that is not from the heart is wrong and this offering would be rejected by God. Trying to compete with others so that we can be in the "in crowd" is also wrong as it would only lead to disaster.

THE SEVEN SONS OF SCEVA

When Paul was in the province of Asia where he had stayed for two years, God did unusual and extraordinary miracles through his ministry. People brought handkerchiefs, towels and aprons to him to pray on and were then taken away and placed upon the sick so that their diseases left them and evil spirits came out of many.

When the seven sons of Sceva, who was a Jewish Chief Priest in the province of Asia, saw the miracles that Paul was performing they decided to copy him by calling upon the name of Jesus Christ over those who had evil spirits as well. Their father saw what they were doing but did not stop them. One day one of the evil spirit replied that it knew Jesus Christ and Paul but that it did not know them; the man who had the evil spirit jumped upon them and beat them up causing them to run out of the room naked and bleeding.

> *"Some Jews who went around driving out evil spirits tried to invoke the name of the Lord Jesus over those who were demon-possessed. They would say, "In the name of Jesus, whom Paul preaches, I command you to come out." Seven sons of Sceva, a Jewish chief priest, were doing this. (One day) the evil spirit answered them, "Jesus I know, and I know about Paul, but who are you?" Then the man who had the evil spirit jumped on them and overpowered them all. He gave them such a beating that they ran out of the house naked and bleeding" (Acts 19:13-16-NIV).*

Trying to drive out evil spirits without first having a personal relationship with Jesus Christ is very dangerous, the fact that these men were the sons of a Jewish chief priest does not mean that salvation could be transferred automatically from their father to them as they had a personal duty to receive Jesus Christ for themselves, they also had a personal duty to revere and honour God.

Their father had a parental duty to bring up his sons in the way of the Lord and to correct and admonish them when necessary.

Proverbs 22:6 states train up your child in the way that he should go so that when he grows up he wouldn't depart from it. It is disheartening that the Chief Priest who led the people of God into worship could not control his children and lead them in the right path. We owe a duty to bring up our children in the way of the Lord so that when they grow up they would not depart from it.

It is disheartening that just like his Predecessors -Aaron, Eli and Samuel - the Chief Priest could not control his children. This problem still persists in the 21st century as we often read and hear of cases in the news of children of renowned Ministers of God acting waywardly and being in trouble with the law.

When you walk in the path God has ordained for you, you won't need to fear what tomorrow will bring as God will order your steps in the right direction. He will give you peace, joy, contentment, satisfaction, happiness, prosperity and good health.

Sometimes it seems easier to take the easy way out in life than comply with God's commandments, rules and regulations. You may get away with your defiance and disobedience in the short term but the consequences of your actions will be with you in the longer term.

To know and to fulfil your purpose in life you must spend time in God's presence. You must spend time in praising and worshipping Him; praying for His promises and studying His Word on a daily basis.

CHAPTER 6   The Next Level with God

A re you ready for the next level in your relationship with God? God is waiting to tell you great and mighty things about your future that you do not yet know of. You will need a fresh encounter with God in order to operate and walk in this new dimension. Rising to a higher dimension in your life and in your relationship with God will require dedication and commitment on your part. It is only when you step up to this higher dimension in your spiritual life that you will begin to see and hear things that will change your playing field.

God wants you to come up higher to where He is; He wants you to climb up higher so that you can change your spiritual altitude. He has opened His door ajar for you to enter and have a discourse with Him, don't waste the opportunity. You can only know what will happen in your future when you step up to hear what the Spirit of God is saying to you.

> *Revelation 4: 1-11 (Amp) says "AFTER THIS I looked, and behold, a door standing open in heaven! And the first voice which I had heard addressing me like [the calling of] a war trumpet said, Come up here, and I will show you what must take place in the future. At once I came under the [Holy] Spirit's power, and behold, a throne stood in heaven, with One seated on the throne! And He Who sat there appeared like [the crystalline brightness of] jasper and [the fiery] sardius, and encircling the throne there was a halo that*

> looked like [a rainbow of] emerald...The twenty-four elders
> (the members of the heavenly Sanhedrin) fall prostrate before
> Him Who is sitting on the throne, and they worship Him Who
> lives forever and ever; and they throw down their crowns
> before the throne, crying out, Worthy are You, our Lord and
> God, to receive the glory and the honour and dominion, for
> You created all things; by Your will they were [brought into
> being] and were created."

To attain this new level in your life where you can commune directly with God you will need to spend time in:-

1. WORSHIPING AND PRAISING GOD

It is good to praise the Lord for He is great and most worthy of our praise. Our God is worthy to receive glory and honour for the good deeds He bestows upon us daily. *Psalm 9:1-2 says "I WILL praise You, O Lord, with my whole heart; I will show forth (recount and tell aloud) all Your marvellous works and wonderful deeds! I will rejoice in You and be in high spirits; I will sing praise to Your name, O Most High!"*

God inhabits the praises of His people, when you praise God you cause Him to rise up and take notice of you. The secret to fulfilling your destiny is praise as praising God will cause Him to move mountains on your behalf. Worshipping and praising God for His past deeds will take you to the next level in life. You must be thankful to God for what He has done in the past. When you think of the victories God has wrought; the dangers He has kept you from and the obstacles He has caused you to surmount, these are sufficient grounds for you to be thankful to Him.

It is by God's favour that He has chosen to establish you as a strong mountain and set your feet on solid rock. You must be thankful to Him for His goodness and mercy towards you and your family; He has traded your sorrow for joy and turned your mourning into dancing.

David said in Psalm 30:12 that his tongue, heart and everything glorious within him will sing praises to the Lord for His wonderful deeds and that he would give thanks to God forever. When we delight ourselves in the Lord He will grant us our innermost desires. The more we commit ourselves to Him, the more God would reward us with good things. You can praise God by making a joyful noise, by clapping, shouting, singing and/or playing instruments.

Thank God for always standing up for you and not giving up on you. Praise Him for the inheritance and blessing He has given to you. Rejoice in all that He has done. When you praise God, He will hasten to accomplish His purpose for your life. Rejoice in the Lord always and sing praises to Him. Never cease singing of God's Mercies and loving kindness for His goodness will continually be felt in your life.

2. PRAYER

Prayer is crucial if you are to become all that God has created you to be. Prayer is the intimate time you have with the Father. Prayer brings about a change in you – in your heart and your life.

The fervent prayer of the righteous can change difficult and impossible situations around. When Prophet Nehemiah heard of the obstacles facing the exiles in rebuilding the walls of Jerusalem he went to the Lord in prayer. He reminded God of His promises and how He had said His plans for Israel would come to pass in their lives if they kept His ordinances and commandments.

Prayer will destroy the covering that satan has been placed over your life which has prevented your glory from shining forth; it will reap away the veil of profound wretchedness that has been woven over you to prevent you from discovering your purpose. Prayer will cause you to take hold of all that God has in store for you and change your testimony. It will wipe away your failures, tears and reproach amongst men. Our God for whom we have waited and hoped on will answer us and save us from all our troubles (*Isaiah 25:7-9*).

In Psalm 102:13, David cried to the Lord to have mercy on him and God answered his prayers. When you cry out to the Lord in prayer, He would hear your cry and come to your aid for help. Prayer reveals God's purpose and will for your life. Some obstacles will not go from your life except by praying and fasting. A praying believer will successfully withstand the strategies of the devil.

Jesus Christ understood the importance of prayer in His ministry, He knew that if He was to succeed in His assignment He needed to set time apart to pray to God to guide and direct Him. On numerous occasions He retired alone, on other occasions he retired with His disciples to pray for the work ahead. If Jesus Christ could take time out to pray and call upon God for strength, why can't we do the same?

Jesus Christ in readiness and anticipation of his crucifixion prayed to His father. He knew that without God strengthening and upholding Him the burden would be too much to bear alone (Matthew 26:36-44). He prayed that God would glorify Him so that He may give eternal life to all whom God had given Him responsibility for. He prayed that God would restore Him to His rightful position where He was before the foundations of the world (John 17).

Jesus prayed for all those who belonged to His fold including you that the Lord would preserve, protect and guard us so that we would accomplish all that God had ordained for us to accomplish. Jesus Christ said the following prayer to God on our behalf:

'Sanctify them [purify, consecrate, separate them for Yourself, make them holy] by the Truth; Your Word is Truth. Just as

You sent Me into the world, I also have sent them into the world. And so for their sake and on their behalf I sanctify (dedicate, consecrate) Myself, that they also may be sanctified (dedicated, consecrated, made holy) in the Truth. Neither for these alone do I pray [it is not for their sake only that I make this request], but also for all those who will ever come to believe in (trust in, cling to, rely on) Me through their word and teaching, That they all may be one, [just] as You, Father, are in Me and I in You, …Father, I desire that they also whom You have entrusted to Me [as Your gift to Me] may be with Me where I am, so that they may see My glory, which You have given Me [Your love gift to Me]; for You loved Me before the foundation of the world"(John 17: 17-24).

God expects you to pray for your family, the Body of Christ, Missionaries and every other person you come across, that they will manifest His purpose in their lives. Prayer will open doors that no man can open for you, Jesus Christ says He has given you the keys of Hades to open and take back all that satan has hidden away from you. Keep praying until you see a change.

3. PLACING YOUR TRUST AND RELIANCE IN GOD

You must trust and rely on God wholeheartedly. You must surrender your life, dreams and aspirations to Him and watch Him transform your life. You must seek God; inquire of Him as your soul's necessity if you are to succeed in life. God's agenda is different from ours, when we run ahead of God, disaster looms.

You must learn to trust in God, as your success in life depends upon it. Despite the trials and tribulations that you may face, remember that God will come through for you and He would take care of things in His own way.

Your trust and reliance upon the Lord will keep you grounded and established despite the torrent, tide or wave that might flow towards you. When you are in anguish God will encompass you to keep you safe and sound. You should never be afraid of what men may do to you, for the Lord is your strength and impenetrable shield. God will empower you to do great exploits when you begin to rely on Him. He will infuse you with an inner strength that you never knew resided within you.

Azariah the son of Oded told King Asa that if he was to succeed, he must forsake every other thing that took the place of God. You must realise that it is only God who can give you total victory. Reliance on your own capabilities and fleshly desires, no matter how attractive will lead to utter destruction (*2 Chronicles 15:1-2*).

Jesus told his disciples that the key to their success was to remain attached to Him. In trying times you must trust and rely on Jesus Christ as your personal Lord and Saviour. You must not allow satan to whisper lies to you that you can make the journey on your own without God. God expects you to dwell and live in Him constantly. He wants you to abide in His love so that your joy and gladness will be in full measure.

> *"I am the true vine, and My Father is the vinedresser... you are the branches. He who abides in Me, and I in him, bears much fruit; for without Me you can do nothing. If anyone does not abide in Me, he is cast out as a branch and is withered; and they gather them and throw them into the fire, and they are burned. If you abide in Me, and My words abide in you, you will ask what you desire, and it shall be done for you. By this My Father is glorified, that you bear much fruit; so you will be My disciples"* John 15:1-8.

Hebrews 13:5k states that God will never leave us nor forsake us; He will never fail us nor leave us without support. He promises that He will be with us till the end of time. From the beginning of creation, God was there, He is here with you today and He will continue to be with you forever.

King David said that he would hand over his life to God alone to whom he trusted, relied upon and was confident in to deliver him from shame and disappointment. He knew that reliance on the shepherd of Israel was profitable for his soul. He knew that the secret to success was to be deeply reliant on God who would prevent him from slipping (*Psalm 25:1-7*). He stated that throughout his life, from his adolescence to old age he had never seen the righteous forsaken by God. God will always come through for the faithful, and deliver us out of every problem.

> *No matter how overwhelming the challenges you may face, remember that God can be relied upon.*

Trusting in the Lord will give you renewed strength and power to mount up and soar like the eagle, you will run and not be wary, you will walk and not faint. You will take on challenging tasks and be successful. Your pace will be different from others as you would have extra lifting power to mount you to greater heights. God will keep in perfect peace those who lean on, trust in and rely upon Him for He will be their everlasting Rock (*Isaiah 40:28-31*).

4. STUDYING THE WORD OF GOD

You must study the scriptures to find and discover the heart of God. Constant meditation on the scriptures will result in you finding answers to the questions no one else can answer. Your thoughts will line up with God's thoughts and your plans will become established. There are many plans in a man's heart but it is God's purpose that will stand. Strive to know Christ on a daily basis, to be intimately acquainted with Him and to understand His ways, *2 Timothy 2:15 (Amp) states that you should "Study and be eager and do your utmost to present yourself to God approved (tested by trial), a workman who has no cause to be ashamed, correctly analyzing and accurately dividing [rightly handling and skilfully teaching] the Word of Truth"*

> *Jeremiah 15:16 (NIV) says "When your words came, I ate them; they were my joy and my heart's delight, for I bear your name, O LORD God Almighty."*

You must study the Word of God to discover what God has in store for you. By searching through the scriptures, God will supply you with abundant wisdom, knowledge and understanding that you will require throughout your life's journey. You will find God's plan and purpose for your life within the scriptures. The fear of the Lord is the beginning of all wisdom (*Deut 7:12-16*).

When you study the word to know God's heart you will begin to see things change for you. You must study God's word because it is the most authentic way to know about Him, it is the most accurate account and explanation of who God is and what He expects from you. God's word will stand the test of time in your life. You must teach your children to study the word of God at an early age so that they will grow to seek Him for themselves in times of trouble.

Moses reminded the children of Israel to bind the statues, commandments and enactments of God in their hearts and that they were to sharpen their minds with the Word of God in case they forget what God had done for them in the past. He also told them to pass on God's word to their next generation so that a true account of God's mercy and faithfulness will be recalled (*Deut 6: 6-12*).

5. OBEYING GOD

Your obedience to God will lead you to becoming prosperous in life. God will reward your commitment and faithfulness by blessing and sanctioning everything you do. Obedience is better than sacrifice, don't sacrifice your soul and your personal standards by going against God's Word; if you truly love God you will obey Him. *Deut 28: 1-2 says "Now it shall come to pass, if you diligently obey the voice of the LORD your God, to observe carefully all His commandments which I command you today; that the LORD your God will set you high above all nations of the earth. And all these blessings shall come upon you and overtake you, because you obey the voice of the LORD your God".*

Moses said blessings would only follow the Israelites if they obeyed and abided by the commandments God had given them. The key to receiving your inheritance in God lies in your obedience to His Word. Disobedience of God's commands could lead to the aborting of one's destiny. **God's blessings are not automatic but conditional upon your obedience;** there are rules and guidelines that need to be followed if you are to become an achiever.

You must live a life worthy of your calling. You cannot go against the will or purpose of God for your life and expect to go the distance. Your behaviour and conduct must be acceptable to God.

6. FORGETTING YESTERDAY'S FAILURES AND MISTAKES

Your failure in the past cannot stop your success in the future. You may think that your past failures dictate the outcome of your future, they don't. You must however understand that your past mistakes were a learning ground to master your skills for the future. We all make mistakes and if anyone thinks he or she is infallible, that person is deceiving him or herself.

You must look forward and forget what has lain behind you, let God free you from the shackles of the past. Lay aside every weight and sin that makes you stumble and look to the past and run with endurance the race that God has called you to. Break the chains of shame, guilt and condemnation from your life as God does not hold you to ransom on account of your past. *Isaiah 1: 18 (NKJV) says "Come now, and let us reason together," Says the LORD, "Though your sins are like scarlet, They shall be as white as snow; Though they are red like crimson, They shall be as wool"*

Although condemnation, guilt and sin may want to hold you back from attaining all that God intends for you to achieve, you should look to Jesus Christ to perfect, correct and strengthen your faith. Jesus Christ atoned your sins and transgressions resulting in God wiping your sins from His sight forever (Romans 3: 24-25), The Holy Spirit has brought us back into right standing with God and has deprived shame of its power; therefore you have absolutely nothing to be ashamed of.

"Stand fast therefore in the liberty by which Christ has made us free, and do not be entangled again with a yoke of bondage" Galatians 5:1.

Learn from your past mistakes and take positive steps to prevent them from recurring. Paul, who referred to himself as a chief sinner made a positive decision to look ahead of him instead of allowing the past failures to choke him. No doubt he had made mistakes which he later regretted but he chose to look forward, ahead of him to better things. You may sometimes remember your past failures and wish you could turn back time, however when you have a clear picture of what you want to achieve and where you want to go you will focus your attention on your destination rather than on your past.

You may be a student who has not been doing too well at school and you are thinking of giving up, don't. The fact that you have been failing your exams and are at the bottom of the class does not mean your future is hopeless. The determining factor is what you do about it to get a change. There were times in our own lives when we felt like failures and that we were a disappointment to God. There were also times when we felt that we were of no earthly use to anyone as we did not appear to be the type who could be entrusted with responsibility.

We were prone to being bottom of our class in our early school days and as there was not much to mark on our exam papers, our teachers resorted to drawing our faces on them instead. They snared at us when we told them what we wanted to become, because in their myopic minds they determined our future by where we were at the time. In fact one of our teachers went further to say that the skies would fall in if we were to pass our GCSEs. When we passed our exams we were tempted to ask her why the skies hadn't come crashing down.

There were other people who laughed and smirked at us to our faces when we told them we wanted to become lawyers when we grew up because they felt we were introverts (which we were at the time) who did not have the ability to speak out, more so speak up to defend anyone! These people felt that we were social outcasts who would forever remain behind closed doors, how they were wrong! If we had allowed people to determine our future, we would have done nothing about pursuing our dream of becoming lawyers.

You may be a divorcee and feel that you are a failure because your marriage did not work out. Instead of feeling sorry for yourself and allowing depression and grief to hold you down, rise up to take on new challenges, you will be surprised at what you can achieve when you focus on new goals. All the negative energy inside you can be channelled to good use. Go out and discover new horizons, you will be surprised at what you may find along the way!

7. FOCUSING AND BEING PURPOSE DRIVEN

You must maintain your focus and not allow peripheral issues to sweep you away from your dominant purpose. God has set your possessions before you, it is time for you to rise up and take possession of them. You must realise that God has already empowered you with all that you would need to attain your goals. You must move out of your comfort zone if you want to see real changes in your life. You cannot keep speaking in tongues that God will bring a change in your life when you are reluctant to take corresponding steps of faith.

You must have a mental picture of where you want to see yourself in the short and long term. Many have forsaken their goals because they had lost momentum or allowed the worries of life to drag them down. It is time to get up, shake off all hindrances; and go back to accomplishing your dream. You must keep your focus on God who is the dominant force in your life and not on others. Shift your focus of yourself and on to God and see what He will do for you.

The Lord told Moses whilst he and the people of Israel were in Horeb that they had dwelt too long in the mountain and that it was time to turn around and continue their journey from where they had left off. In turn Moses reminded the children of Israel to take heed and guard their lives diligently so as to not forget the things their eyes had seen.

> *'The LORD our God spoke to us in Horeb, saying: 'You have dwelt long enough at this mountain. Turn and take your journey, and go to the mountains of the Amorites, to all the neighbouring places in the plain, in the mountains and in the lowland, in the South and on the seacoast, to the land of the Canaanites and to Lebanon, as far as the great river, the River Euphrates. See, I have set the land before you; go in and possess the land which the LORD swore to your fathers—to Abraham, Isaac, and Jacob—to give to them and their descendants after them" Deut 1:6-8.*

In the 2001 Epic film, "**A Knight's Tale**"[2] Heath Ledger stars as a lowly squire who jousts his way to the top in medieval Europe. When he was growing up, he told his father that he dreamt that he

---

[2] **A Knight's Tale** (2001) is a film written and directed by Brian Helgeland.

would one day become a Knight; this was an impossible aspiration by many of his time as it was not possible to change one's status but with sheer determination, drive and focus, the squire became a knight.

For some, maintaining the right focus is easy whilst for others it is hard work. The consequences of losing the right focus can be costly. There were a number of men in the Bible who started their journey in life well but once they achieved minimal success they allowed themselves to become distracted from their calling and lost their mark. Some of these men were:-

a) **Jehoshaphat** who reigned after his father, King Asa. In the beginning Jehoshaphat sought after the Lord who established his kingdom in reward for his commitment. He took away the high places and the Asherim out of Judah and his neighbours feared him. God prospered and increased him because of his drive and commitment towards the Lord's house (2 Chronicles 17: 1-6), however later,

I) He became idle, lost his focus and went down to King Ahab in Samaria who killed sheep and oxen for him and his people. King Ahab also persuaded him to go up against Ramoth-gilead. On his return to Jerusalem, Jehu the Seer reprimanded and rebuked him for helping the ungodly, and for loving those who hated the Lord, God pardoned him on this occasion because good deeds were found within him (2 Chronicles 19:2-3).

ii) He became a busybody by joining King Ahaziah of Israel to build ships to go to Tarshish. He was rebuked by Prophet Eliezer, who informed him that God would nullify his good works (2 Chronicles 20:37).

b) **King Joash** of Jerusalem became a king at 7 years of age when he replaced Athaliah his grandmother. He kept his focus during the days of Jehoiada, the priest who was his uncle, but once Jehoiada died, King Joash aligned himself to the Princes of Judah and he forsook his God, choosing to worship idols instead. When

Zechariah, the priest rebuked him for his loss of focus, King Joash commanded that he be killed in the court of the Lord's House. King Joash in turn was killed by his own servants on his bed whilst sick (2 Chronicles 24).

c) **King Uzziah** was 16 years old when he began his reign in Jerusalem under the guidance of Zechariah who instructed him in the Way of the Lord. He carried out building projects; built an array of army which he strengthened and equipped and defeated his enemies. However, like many Kings before him he lost his focus when he became strong, he became proud and refused to listen to Azariah, the priest's counsel who rebuked him for entering the Temple to burn incense on the Altar. King Uzziah became enraged that he was corrected; he became cursed and died a leper.

> *"But when he was strong his heart was lifted up, to his destruction, for he transgressed against the LORD his God by entering the temple of the LORD to burn incense on the altar of incense. So Azariah the priest went in after him, and with him were eighty priests of the LORD—valiant men. And they withstood King Uzziah, and said to him, "It is not for you, Uzziah, to burn incense to the LORD, but for the priests, the sons of Aaron, who are consecrated to burn incense. Get out of the sanctuary, for you have trespassed! You shall have no honour from the LORD God." Then Uzziah became furious; and he had a censer in his hand to burn incense. And while he was angry with the priests, leprosy broke out on his forehead, before the priests in the house of the LORD, beside the incense altar.' 2 chronicle 26:16-19.*

d) **King Hezekiah** after recovering from his illness received the messengers of Merodach-Baladan, King of Babylon into his palace where he showed them his entire possessions. He showed them the house of his armour, jewels and treasures of silver and gold. Prophet Isaiah rebuked Hezekiah for glorying in his possessions and told him that the King of Babylon would return to take his sons away into captivity (Isaiah 39).

For you to be productive, you must maintain your focus at all times. You do not want to start well, expend all the effort, resources and time on your dreams and goals only to abort them along the way. You must be diligent so that satan does not steal your joy at the end. Take stock of where you are, what you are doing and where you want to finish and keep this map in front of you always. It is not always easy keeping the right focus when life's challenges come your way as they have a way of making you go off course. However, when you lose your focus, re-charge yourself up and continue from where you left off, slowly, surely and steadily you will accomplish your purpose.

8. CASTING AWAY UNBELIEF

Unbelief will hinder the move of God in your life and it will stifle the growth of the Holy Spirit in you. You must cast down every vain imagination and every word that elevates itself above the knowledge of God. Refuse the lies of the devil that says that you do not have the ability to achieve your purpose.

Faith without works is dead faith. God must see the works of your faith before He can move mountains on your behalf. Unbelief would prevent God performing miracles in your life. Don't allow unbelief to destroy your future, when you notice any root of unbelief in your life you must deal with it immediately so that it does not become malignant and grow to destroy every seed of faith that had germinated in your life.

'And these attesting signs will accompany those who believe: in My name they will drive out demons; they will speak in new languages; They will pick up serpents; and [even] if they drink anything deadly, it will not hurt them; they will lay their hands on the sick, and they will get well. So then

*the Lord Jesus, after He had spoken to them, was taken up
into heaven and He sat down at the right hand of God. And
they went out and preached everywhere, while the Lord
kept working with them and confirming the message by the
attesting signs and miracles that closely accompanied [it].
Amen (so be it)." (Mark 16:17-20-Amp).*

9. TAKING POSITIVE ACTION

You must take positive action if you want to achieve good success. Whilst taking this positive action, it must also be Godly. There is no point in saying that you are inspired to succeed when you are sitting on your backside. You have to get up from your slumber and take positive steps. Your words and actions must be in consonance with each other. It is not enough for you to claim your possessions by word of mouth; you must take physical action to possess what God has in store for you. There is nothing wrong with positive confession but this alone is not sufficient if you are to reach greater heights for Jesus Christ. The accomplishment of your destiny is not dependent on anyone else but yourself.

Instead of waiting for circumstances to be conducive, seize the moment and maximise the time allotted to you. Don't wait until you feel inspired to take action rather ask the Holy Spirit to guide you on your journey. You should utilize your time by grasping each opportunity that comes your way.

Despite Israel's victory over their enemies in the Promised Land they failed to occupy the whole land God had for them. They failed to drive out the Jebusites, the original inhabitants of Jerusalem, dwelling side by side with them until these people became a snare to them (Joshua 15:63).

Unlike the Israelites before them, Nehemiah and his supporters laboured at the work of building the temple. Despite the opposition, Nehemiah pursued the goal of rebuilding the Temple of God by engaging and motivating the Israelites, his actions ensured that the Temple was rebuilt in fifty two days"

> *"From that day on, half of my men did the work, while the other half were equipped with spears, shields, bows and armour. The officers posted themselves behind all the people of Judah who were building the wall. Those who carried materials did their work with one hand and held a weapon in the other, and each of the builders wore his sword at his side as he worked". But the man who sounded the trumpet stayed with me..." (Nehemiah 4: 16-18 NIV).*

In 1940, in his first address as the newly appointed Prime Minister of the United Kingdom, **Sir Winston Churchill**[3] said the following concerning taking action,

> *".... You ask, what is our policy? I will say; 'It is to wage war, by sea, land and air, with all our might and with all the strength that God can give us: ... That is our policy.' You ask, what is our aim? I can answer with one word: Victory - victory at all costs, victory in spite of all terror, victory however long and hard the road may be; for without victory there is no survival."*

He also made the following comments-

> *"Never give in—never, never, never, never, in nothing great or small, large or petty, never give in except to convictions of honour and good sense. Never yield to force; never yield to the apparently overwhelming might of the enemy"*

> *"Every day you may make progress. Every step may be fruitful. Yet there will stretch out before you an ever-lengthening, ever-ascending, ever-improving path... But this, so far from discouraging, only adds to the joy and glory of the climb".*

---

[3] The Wit & Wisdom of Winston Churchill by James C. Humes and Richard M Nixon.

"It is no use saying, "We are doing our best." You have got to succeed in doing what is necessary"

"We shall not fail or falter; we shall not weaken or tire...Give us the tools and we will finish the job".

10. SEEKING GUIDANCE AND MENTORSHIP

You need the Holy Spirit to guide and direct your steps. Jesus assured us that He would send His Holy Spirit, the Counsellor, Comforter, and Advocate who would direct us and lead us on the right path. The Holy Spirit is our number one guide who would prevent our foot from slipping.

You would also require the counsel and mentorship of others who have gone before you. You would need others to guide you into taking great strides to your destination. The Body of Christ needs those who would help strengthen those who have been weakened by the trials of life. To achieve your goals, you must be truthful about your weaknesses and strengths. You may need additional training, assistance or counselling to improve certain areas of your life.

Some good examples of mentor/protégé relationships recorded in the Bible are those between Elijah and Elisha, Moses and Joshua, Apostle Paul and Timothy, Priscilla/ Aquila and Appollos and Jesus Christ and His Disciples. By taking counsel from others you will shorten the time it takes you to do things.

Isaac *Newton said this adage "If I have seen farther than others, it is because I was standing on the shoulders of giants."*

When Jethro, Moses' father-in-law noticed that Moses was attending to the people of Israel all day long he told Moses to nominate people to assist him in alleviating his workload so that Moses would not suffer a burnout. Jethro provided fatherly counsel to

Moses and introduced the concept of time management, which Moses clearly lacked.

> *"Moreover, you shall choose able men from all the people—God-fearing men of truth who hate unjust gain—and place them over thousands, hundreds, fifties, and tens, to be their rulers. And let them judge the people at all times; every great matter they shall bring to you, but every small matter they shall judge. So it will be easier for you, and they will bear the burden with you. If you will do this, and God so commands you, you will be able to endure [the strain], and all these people also will go to their [tents] in peace. So Moses listened to and heeded the voice of his father-in-law and did all that he had said. Moses chose able men out of all Israel and made them heads over the people, rulers of thousands, of hundreds, of fifties, and of tens. And they judged the people at all times; the hard cases they brought to Moses, but every small matter they decided themselves" (Exodus 18:21-26-Amp).*

By taking Jethro's advice on board, Moses showed that he was able to accept constructive criticism; he was able to improve his effectiveness thereby leaving him with more time to serve and hear from God.

In Acts 6:1-7, Peter followed the advice of the Apostles when the Hellenists, who were the Greek speaking Jews, complained to Peter and the Apostles that their widows were being overlooked. The Apostles delegated some of their responsibilities to able and trustworthy elders who were selected from the brethren to conduct the pressing daily affairs; as a result the Apostles had more time on their hands to focus on their main objectives of soul winning and building the spiritual lives of their followers.

CHAPTER 7

Called to Your Purpose

Become An Eagle Believer And Dominate The Skyline

The Eagle is a symbol of greatness, majesty and valance; the undisputed champion of the sky, what can rival it in its flight. The Eagle was designed, arrayed and clothed with dignity to soar and conquer its rivals!

Just observe the ways of the eagle in the sky; they are symbolic, majestic and awesome.

The eagle's frame suits its assignment: to fly and soar high come rain or sunshine,

God has created you to become an 'Eagle Believer', a person of outstanding ability, character and dignity to dominate life's skyline!

So dominate life's challenges as a valiant warrior because you are an 'Eagle Believer'.

Either Take The Plunge Or Remain Afraid And Be a Mediocre

You must understand that Rome was not built in a day. The architects who designed and built the empire of success began in the drawing room and in the amphitheatre where they defended their beliefs and convictions to win their opponents over.

You must take the plunge and step out on to the pavement of life, take the plunge by being a pace setter instead of remaining afraid and being a mediocre.

Mediocrity and fear originate from the belief that it is not possible to break out of the mould of yesterday to venture into the future.

You must rise out of your comfort zone to break the barriers of fear and stagnation.

Hone Your Skills To Have The Master Stroke

Michelangelo Buonarroti with his stroke became the greatest artist, painter and sculptor.

Luciano Pavarotti with his voice became a master performer and touched the right notes.

Albert Einstein with his mind became a scientific and mathematical genius.

They became Maestros because they worked day and night to master their craft. What are you doing with your skill? The world will not seek after what is common but what is uncommon.

Maestros are rare and they command/court the attention of royalty and nobility, whilst the mediocre are common and command the attention of only their peers.

Hone your God-given skills to make them perfect, so that with the Master Stroke you can shine.

Have a Little Patience On The Way To where You Are Going

In your journey to your destination, you may feel disappointed that you are not moving as fast as you would like or as quickly as you ought to do.

You must learn not to over-do things or to run ahead of your better judgement. Having a little patience will ensure that you have time to review your goals, reflect on the actions you want to take and have time to manoeuvre before committing yourself fully.

Don't act on a "last opportunity or chance" basis which you think will elude you if you don't act immediately because acting on impulse may cost you dearly.

Having a little patience could save you time, money and sleepless nights! Don't judge your progress in life by others around you. Set your own pace, be patient and allow God to do His magnificent work in and through you.

Critics Are Short Sighted about Your Purpose

You are the only one who can stop yourself from reaching the top of the ladder. Your opponents might have told you that you wouldn't make it, give yourself credit for how far you've come.

Your critics would have their say, but they can't stop your dreams from coming to pass. Your family, friends and foes may not believe that you have the grit to go all the way — but just wait until they see you shine.

Remember that critics are short sighted as they see dimly through a darkened mirror about what they believe you might become, but your destiny is not in their hands.

Just take a good look at yourself, with sheer determination and faith; you will achieve your purpose.

Every Little Step Counts

No matter how small or insignificant each step you take in life appears to be, know that these steps collectively will enable you to get closer to your goals of spiritual, emotional and financial freedom.

These little steps are subjective and relative. To one person it might be insignificant whilst to another it might be of great importance.

So take that extra tutorial or attend that evening class, save that extra dollar/pound; invest in property/real estate; take a course in Internet Marketing or join a public speaking class to build up your moral/ social relationships. You never know where these little steps will take you!

We want you to know that these little steps will certainly take you closer to your destination and the fulfilment of your God given purpose.

Success takes One Day at a Time

If you often wonder why you have failed to achieve all that you set out to achieve, it may be because you are not taking it one day at a time.

If you must succeed at all, you must do what the ancients did in the days gone by - one day at a time to build up yourself.

Today is a new day with new challenges. Tap into your inner strength in order to cope with what life throws at you.

Overcoming challenges means: staying in the ring to finish the fight, never falling on the count but remaining strong to survive the last count, we know you too will succeed; it just takes a day at a time.

It does not matter how you start the day but how you utilise the hours in the day; you must overcome what life throws at you so that when you lay your head down at night you can truly say- "I won the day."

> *What do you aspire to achieve? Take it one day at a time and you will reach your destination.*

CHAPTER 8

Your Life Destination

Travel the Path No One has Tread

To be unique you must be willing to travel the path no one has dared travel before. You have to separate yourself from others if you want to be known as the pearl out of the oyster that became the prized object which kings, queens and nobility sought after.

Pearls come in a variety of colours; the most expensive is the natural pearl, which takes time to be formed just like you. The oyster chose to do the things that challenged it and tread the path no other oyster has dared to tread in order to produce the natural pearl.

It is said that cultured pearls are generally less expensive because they aren't as rare as natural pearls, God intended you to be an original, don't become a carbon copy!

Unmerited Favour is... God's Grace and Mercy

Once God knows that you are serious about Him, He will pave your journey with His Grace and Mercy.

God's unmerited favour is without limit; His favour will cause you to reach the top with little effort.

God's grace and mercy is surely needed throughout your life's journey, so seek Him earnestly and you would have a good dosage of His unmerited favour.

Jesus Christ apportioned His Grace to us to empower us to do the work of the Ministry for edifying of the Body of Christ.

Don't Allow Fear of Succeeding Prevent You from Starting Out on Your Journey

It is one thing to be afraid of failure, but it is another to be afraid of success. Fear of success prevents many from starting out on their journey into their destiny.

If you wonder whether the fear of success truly exists, check out those who refuse to take a promotion for fear that they will be thrown into the limelight or asked to take the stand.

You must trust that God who has called you will put out His Hand to steady you up on your journey to success.

Don't Waste Your Time Wishing You'd Turned Back Time!

Time is what you make of it: time could be love, money or trust.

Looking backwards would waste you time especially when you know you cannot turn back time. However, you have the opportunity to learn from past mistakes and move ahead to better times.

So don't wish you could turn back time and waste more of your time and everybody's time!

Aspire To Greater Heights

It is not wrong for you to want to aspire beyond your current station in life- whatever that may be! You hold the wheel of fortune in your hands and only you can spin the wheel and throw the dice in your favour.

Some people were born into affluence but squandered their fortune away and failed to pass on their wealth to their next generation. Others were born into obscurity but aspired to greater heights and left the shores of life impacting their next generation, while a third preferred to remain where they were, as they believed in fate instead of faith.

We have learned to aspire to greater heights because we know that we will have the opportunity of imparting our generation and leaving our mark on the shores of infinity! It is only the short sighted who say we should remain where we are instead of aspiring to greater heights.

A Day Closer to your Destination

The journey may be slow, the path may be narrow, the mountains high and the valley deep but we can see beyond the highest mountain to the level crossing of life now.

You may have backtracked some days, months or years and lost time in the process but know that it only takes a twinkling of an eye for things to change and for you to be closer to your destination.

The same goes for those who may have planned their life's journey for years but find out that it takes only a second for them to find themselves where they want to be.

Journey of Life – Our Testimony

We have looked at the progress we have made in life thus far … it has not been by sheer will power alone but by the help of God in Heaven who has sustained us thus far. We remember being told that we would not amount to anything. Oh how we wish that those who had little hope about our future could see us now!

Ours is a journey of life. It doesn't matter how or where we started but rather how well we complete the race of life. We must not allow restrictions of any sort curtail or stop our journey.

Do you know that we once thought that we were useless? We copied what other people did – in our manner of dressing, walking and talking amongst others as we did not have our own conviction. We wanted to be like other people whom we thought had it all together; in the process we lost our own identity and began to conform to other peoples' expectations of us. We had developed a lock-step mentality! We lost focus of where we wanted to go and what we wanted to do. We had simply lost the plot!

The defining moment in our lives came in 1996 when our spiritual mentor gave us a tract to read entitled "Who I Am in God". As we read through the scriptures mentioned in the tract we began to see ourselves as God saw us. We also began to see our lives transformed from the "inside out". We began to accept ourselves for who God had created us to be. We stopped being a carbon copy of others. It was enough that there were two of us (as we are twins), we did not need to be clones of others!

Following on from this, we began to pursue God's vision and calling for our individual lives. We began to do the things we didn't have the courage to do as we understood that we could now do all things through Christ who strengthens us. We became assertive, confident and less introverted; and to be at peace with ourselves.

You see we had wrongly believed that we were incomplete without "certain people" in our lives and that by associating with these people we will be complete. We soon discovered our self-deceit and became disillusioned that we had built idols in our lives for years that could not satisfy the yearnings in our spirit and heart. We now know that we can only find our true identity in Christ and He is the One who completes us. He is the <u>Pillar that holds our lives</u> in place.

We discovered that our greatest error was not understanding and appreciating that all we ever needed is Jesus Christ, who is the "only Solid Rock" on which we stand. We realised that our foundation needed to be built on Jesus Christ as all other ground is sinking sand. We realised that we could only make the journey of life with Christ at the helm of our lives. We let go of all the shackles (bitterness, un-forgiveness, hatred, anger and insecurities) that had hitherto plagued our lives. By His Grace we have moved on to take hold of all the blessings He has in store for us.

> *Sheer willpower would not take you to your life's destination; only Christ can!*

Conclusion

May you prosper in every way- body, soul and spirit as you begin your journey into your destiny and may God's mercy, peace and love be multiplied and bestowed bountifully upon you.

As you overcome and obey God's commands to become all that He has ordained you to be, He will give you authority and power to rule over the nations and become a pillar in His sanctuary. God will grant you permission to sit beside Him in His throne just as Jesus Christ was granted that permission. Revelation 3:5 says that he who overcomes shall be clothed in white garment and He will not blot out his name from the Book of Life.

You must not leave this world full of untapped resources. Rather, you must achieve your assignment so that after your departure your achievements will be spoken of before God, and by men whom you have touched with your life. You cannot afford to delay or procrastinate any longer; whilst there is still light you must tarry to fulfil your purpose. God ordained and sanctified you to accomplish purpose through Him.

Jesus Christ was considered worthy and deserving to open the scroll in heaven because He had accomplished the purpose and assignment that was given to Him. He was called the Lion of the tribe of Judah and became the leader of His flock; you also must live up to the name God has given you.

A new song was sung in heaven for Jesus Christ because He had done what no one else did. He purchased you to become a kingdom and priest to God to reign supreme over the earth, therefore you have been empowered by God to rise up from your current position to reign over the affairs of life.

The old heaven and old earth passed away to make room for the new. God will wipe away every tear from your eyes and He will make all things become new for you. He is the Alpha and Omega — the Beginning and the End. God is saying to you that He is the beginning and end of your life. He who formed you from the very beginning will surely pave your end with gold.

You may think you have failed yourself, the people around you and God; however, God is saying that your old sins and mistakes were in your yesterday. He has thrown all your failures and negative feelings into the sea of forgetfulness never to be remembered again. Do you have a hunger and thirst which people or things can't fill? We want you to know that this hunger and thirst you have is actually a longing for God.

God says to those who are thirsty He will give sparkling water flowing from the fountain of the water of life. The water will strengthen, refresh and satisfy you and you will never want again. This water will wash away every curse, impurity, hatred, sin, bitterness and offence that is holding you back in life. God says He will fill your thirst and hunger with His goodness (Psalm 107:9).

We pray that you will begin to operate in your calling all the days of your life from now onwards — in Jesus Christ's Name.

Thanks so much for reading this book. We hope you enjoyed it and have come to know who God has created you to be from the beginning of your conception.

We pray that God's blessings, Grace and Spirit will be bestowed upon you and that you receive revelation from Him of Who He is, who He has created you to be and the bright future He has in store for you.

If you have found this book helpful, kindly provide your reviews on the website you purchased a copy of this book from or the various publishing platforms such as Amazon, CreateSpace and Lulu.

Other Books by Authors

Hearing God's Voice

You Are Blessed

The Beginners' Guide to Wealth Creation

A Simple Guide to UK Immigration

The Beginners' Guide to Writing, Self-Publishing and Marketing a Book

Purpose2Destiny TK Limited
P O BOX 3162
Romford
RM3 9WR
United Kingdom

www.ingramcontent.com/pod-product-compliance
Lightning Source LLC
Chambersburg PA
CBHW060922040426
42445CB00011B/738